FACING THE TORTURER

Other books by François Bizot

The Gate
Le Saut de Varan

FACING THE TORTURER

TORTURER

INSIDE THE MIND OF A WAR CRIMINAL

François Bizot

*translated by Charlotte Mandell
and Antoine Audouard*

RIDER

LONDON · SYDNEY · AUCKLAND · JOHANNESBURG

1 3 5 7 9 10 8 6 4 2

First published in the UK in 2012 by Rider, an imprint of Ebury Publishing
Published in France in 2011 as *Le silence du bourreau* by Flammarion

Ebury Publishing is a Random House Group company

The Random House Group Limited Reg. No. 954009

Addresses for companies within the Random House Group can be found at:
www.randomhouse.co.uk

A CIP catalogue record for this book is available from the British Library

The Random House Group Limited supports The Forest
Stewardship Council (FSC®), the leading international forest
certification organisation. Our books carrying the FSC label are
printed on FSC® certified paper. FSC is the only forest certification
scheme endorsed by the leading environmental organisations,
including Greenpeace. Our paper procurement policy can be found at:
www.randomhouse.co.uk/environment

Printed and bound by CPI Group (UK) Ltd, Croydon, CR0 4YY

ISBN: 9781846042553 (hardback)
ISBN: 9781846043277 (paperback)

Copies are available at special rates or bulk orders. Contact the sales
development team on 020 7840 8487 for more information.

To buy books by your favourite authors and register for offers, visit
www.randomhouse.co.uk

In fact, 'recognising' someone – and even more, after being unable to recognise him, identifying him – is thinking of two contradictory things under the same name; it's acknowledging that the one who had been the person one remembers no longer exists, and that the one who is there is a person one no longer knows; it's having to think of a mystery almost as disturbing as the mystery of death of which it is, as it were, the preface and the forerunner. . . .

Marcel Proust, *Time Regained*

If I were placed in front of that effigy
Unknown to myself, not knowing my own features,
From all the ghastly folds of anguish and energy
I would read my torments, and recognise myself.

Paul Valéry, *Mélange*

Contents

Phnom Penh, 8 May 2009

——*Mr François Bizot, can you describe what you saw at the M-13 Security Camp during your detention there, up until your release and return to Phnom Penh?*

—— *Certainly, your Honour. Nevertheless, I would like to start with one of the final events from my detention at the M-13 Camp. On the eve of my liberation – 24 December 1971 – I was authorised by the accused, Duch, to organise a farewell dinner for my fellow prisoners, tethered together to rods. I carried them bowls of chicken soup, bought with the money that had been confiscated from me at the time of my arrest. I went to each of them. Those who dared to talk to me, said: 'French comrade! Please don't forget us'.*

Today it's Duch who is accused and he is the one bound to the bar, so to speak. On this occasion may I evoke the memory of the M-13 prisoners, who I never stop thinking of, in particular my two assistants, Ung Hok Lay and Kang Son, who were later executed in another camp, because they had worked with me.

It is in their name that I wish to testify today.

PART ONE

I.

1963 – Sarah

'Bar-le-Duc! Bar-le-Duc! Eight-minute stop.'

A train is arriving in a station – like a wheel of fortune at the end of its spin: the sequence of images slowing down, the window cutting a random frame. I remember the scene as if it were yesterday. The twilight already held the cold of autumn fog. An icy drizzle reflected the light of the bulbs through to the end of the platform. From there ran a ramp that led to the track. I didn't know yet that I would soon slip on to it to reach the ballast. That night, my life stopped for the first time.

I was with my mother; my father had just died, we were going to visit my sister. Sarah had taken refuge in my arms, worried by the noise. She had hardly ever gone out since I'd brought her back from the Colom-Béchard garrison in Algeria and entrusted her to my parents. With her big angular ears, her smouldering eyes, her bushy tail, her wild instinct – she sniffed everything with her tiny muzzle, ready to jump and escape at any moment.

She was the prettiest thing. I would have fought for her. The habits of my comrades in the 711th Signal Corps Division were familiar to me, but hers were even more so, down to her oddest whims. At night, I would take off her collar and we would sleep in the sand under the same blanket. After my military service, I had remained so attached to her that my father kindly took care of her while I went off travelling. He kept her with him in his office, under the drawing table, where he had placed a piece of linoleum that she dug into, yapping, as if it were her burrow. She calmed down in his presence but would bite my mother's fingers.

'What are we going to do with the little fennec now? I don't know how I'll be able to look after her all alone,' my mother said abruptly as we were leaving the cemetery.

In the blink of an eye, I slipped away into the cold of the railway station. I had noticed that the narrow passageway leading down from the platform went along a track that was out of earshot from the surroundings. I remember imagining the look of puzzlement on the faces of railwaymen who would, sooner or later, come across her soft blond fur. I fled back, as if emerging from a cesspool, still reeling in vile disgust at what I had just done – a mixture of impressions, brute force, defiance and horror, all magnified by my father's death – my eyes welling with tears.

As I write these lines, I am once again overcome by the same repugnance; that day, my confidence was shattered, and it was shattered for ever.

My mother didn't have to look twice to notice the blood on the sleeve of my raincoat. I felt her eyes rest on me, focus on different parts of my face, as if to discover someone, to take the measure of the man I had become, and perhaps too, poor woman, of her own responsibility in what she was beginning to understand.

Even while my father was still alive, it was clear that I would not stay in France: the beginnings of the life I dreamed of, for which I was eager to change everything, did not lie there. I calmly embraced this desire as a natural urge to go far away into one of those unknown countries that everyone bears within themselves; I was still dazzled by the creative selfishness my childhood had been immersed in, I was shameless, ready for anything.

Back in the shadows of the train, realising that my mother couldn't look after Sarah, and that my departure was unavoidable – it was an escape to which I clung with every fibre of my being – I considered the pros and cons of my crime, till I regarded it as a necessary and in the end courageous sacrifice. It was up to me to resolve a problem to which no one else could find a solution. As for letting myself off lightly by selling Sarah – during the Algerian War a sand fox was a fashionable pet – the very idea seemed degrading and weak: you only sell things that don't matter.

Sarah mattered. Sacrificing her was not, in my eyes, a minor crime; far from it. The little animal shared the behavioural traits of all living beings – fear, aggression, a need to nest. Mine was in no way a slight or trivial action; it grew from a resolution no less serious than if I had decided to kill a person. I was convinced that it had been just as difficult to create the fennec as it had been the *Homo sapiens*. Without much feeling, I had already witnessed from afar the deaths of a good handful of men of my age, chosen with indifference. In war, isn't it the duty of men to kill their brethren? This had cured me of the belief in any supremacy of human beings; I'd lost any illusion that they, alone, were endowed with a soul, with a spiritual life. It seemed to me that the value of each living being could be viewed as in direct proportion to the amount of suffering one felt in losing it. How could the death of a little pampered, humanised animal – which I pictured emerging from the same layers of the universe as me – affect me less than the death of a complete stranger whom I had no reason to love?

*

General de Gaulle did not allow the hens from his chicken coop to be served to him, because every morning, during his walk in Colombey-les-deux-Églises, he watched them scratch about in the grass as he went by, and thus saw them live. It was the same with me: I could only remain indifferent to the slaughter of an animal if I had never seen it before.

At the time all children had a patron saint. Mine was Francis of Assisi and I was proud of my protector. I fought, as he did, for the integration of all creatures, in a kind of bill of rights for living beings. At my first communion I was given pictures of the wolf of Gubbio and of the Sermon to the Birds; for me, there was no clear-cut separation between the world of animals and our own, and I worshipped the invisible, spiritual, presence that I felt living within them. Though science and philosophy after St Francis insisted on the radical difference between men endowed with reason and 'animal-machines', I never felt foreign to the animal kingdom.

My feelings have not changed since then. This way of dividing the living world saddens me. It remains one of the limits, one of the thresholds that I have never been able to cross.

When I arrived in Cambodia in 1965, I silently saw, as everyone else did, live turtles being flipped on the grill; the backs of otters gashed open with machetes in order to keep their fetters intact; the bloody snouts of pigs tied to racks rubbing against the road – every animal a victim of our indifference, of this detachment that separates man from the others, the same detachment that allowed the Khmer Rouge to smash babies' heads against a tree or wall.

When we kill, let's say, 'because we have to', the important thing is our way of seeing and thinking at that moment – our way of sensing the forbidden, the weight of the danger – without explanation. In the same way, after World War II, I had quickly understood that the meat that rationing had deprived us of for so long was also somehow taboo.

We were living in Nancy then. When I went to the Essey stadium with my father, we would avoid passing by the slaughterhouses, whose stench invaded my child's brain. I could vaguely sense what it was they did there, even if I was unable to imagine for a second what the walls of that closed empire actually concealed. Later on, the rumour that a multitude of dehumanised people, mostly Jews, had been led to slaughter reached me surrounded by the same aura of mystery – did they have no souls either?

I always remember a conversation with my father in around 1954. We'd just left the cigarette shop that was on the corner, across from the brasserie d'Amerval. He had told me that in the beginning living beings had appeared under water. They had left the water to go on land, and then, as they evolved, had managed to fly into the air. We had agreed that this was Progress – the evolution of life, in several stages, from low to high, towards an ideal end. But some of these creatures, too attracted by the low, had only managed to raise themselves up by clinging to trees.

This group included the most intelligent beings, and most of its members had quickly decided to return to ground, with the aim of building their empire there, even if it meant living as carnivores, and paying a high price for their situation. Their trick was to make their foolishness appear inspired. We, mankind, were their faithful heirs. From that moment on, nothing survived on earth, below ground or in the water that these beings didn't track down, fool, chase and destroy. Everything had to submit to the voracity of their desire.

Only the birds had escaped this domination, by flying swiftly away, with the splendid lightness of their feathered wings, while the other species had been deprived of their rights. The invention of knowledge, like that of good and evil, dated from that time. Birds had become the only creatures able to dive deeply into the very dream of life, to exist peacefully, far from the world and from gods, at a distance from the human species, from the killing fields and other concentration camps.

Presumptuous and immoderate, men had also tried repeatedly to reach the skies, but the too-great weight of their limbs would bring them back to earth. This tension within them, between weight and lightness, became the most tragic aspect of their condition down below. Since then, the idea of going to the great beyond, to the place where birds disappear, swallowed by the sky, has become the sole goal that they pursue without ever attaining it.

To my child's mind, this tale said it all: this was why men had endowed angels with wings and why, with their souls debased by their own weight, they were eternally striving for the myth of a lost paradise, whose path to heaven they continually sought.

Like every time in those moments when I walked alongside my father, feeling his hand gently resting on my shoulder, I had the feeling that these words were engraving themselves in my memory, forging what would later become my first adult thoughts.

*

A number of Germans were garrisoned in Nancy, where the rumour of an Allied landing was already gaining ground. I was walking with my mother up the wide path of the Pépinière Gardens, which led to the old oaks of the playground. A little way off, an SS officer was approaching us. When we came even with him, I stuck my tongue out at him. The officer stood stock-still. My mother, frightened, immediately gave me a sharp slap.

'Madame, why do you hit your son? If I were you, I would be proud of him,' he said in French, with a click of his heels, before continuing on his way.

That day, from the example of my mother who rarely hit me, and never as hard as that, I understood that fear could push anyone beyond the normal limits of their behaviour.

In the following years, I often heard my parents recount that scene. When we had guests, my father would affect an air of surprise each time before beginning it; and he liked to call attention to the moral of the story which, aside from a few notions about the ardour of my budding patriotism, wasn't necessarily what everyone had been expecting.

That was my first encounter with a thought that would grow within me over time: even though people were – or precisely because they were – full of good intentions, they could find themselves mixed up in criminal undertakings. To fight them was a necessity that followed a set of rules: a true spirit of resistance forbade any compromise with an enemy officer, however likeable he might seem.

After the Liberation of France, the first books I read told of the adventures of merchants who went to buy slaves in order to resell them like animals in markets. I was revolted by the right they claimed to mistreat their bounty, under the pretext of its animal nature.

Slavery had been shaking humanity since prehistoric times; it took advantage of the use we made of beasts; just as, if I understood rightly, mass crimes had copied their procedures from those of slaughterhouses. A link was growing gradually in my mind between these two realities. How could you not believe that one was the result of the other; that one would not follow on from the other? Some crimes, it seems, affect humanity as a whole, in its very structure and *raison d'être*.

Looking at things in this way – from a biological perspective – can be disconcerting and lead to a very pessimistic view of man. But this child's view – the most implacable of all the gazes we direct at ourselves – doesn't last long; the fear that surreptitiously wells up in us no longer reaches our collective awareness. I hoped but dared not believe that banning slaughter – in Nancy they killed mostly with poleaxes and by exsanguination – might be the only way to remove from man the wish to devour others, and to enslave others to build empires; to make them disgusted with it by killing the very instinct at its root. For me, the eating of animal flesh became the telltale sign of a death wish, the symbol of a progressive devouring of ourselves, to the point of autophagy.

I thought that we would one day come to remember slaughterhouses as the mark of another age, with the same shame with which we remember the slave trade. Regarding the definition and limits of other, non-human, living beings my imagination has hardly gone beyond those initial intuitions. But I found the idea wonderful that man has descended from apes. One of my ancestors had ventured forth, leaving the virtuous shade of the tall trees, and imposed his rule by subjugating other creatures: this allowed me to better understand 'what we are here below'.[1]

*

We didn't talk about these things amongst ourselves, but I observed later, in Algeria, that the hearts of my regimental comrades weren't much more sensitive than my own when faced with the body of a *fellah*, a local peasant, whereas we were devastated by the death of a comrade we were used to seeing, moved by feelings that could sometimes be surprising, like the ones now that made me cry in the train. I bewailed my fate, overcome by my shameful act: I had sacrificed Sarah in order to purge myself of the repercussions of my father's death. But killing her without its being viewed as morally wrong, without incurring any punishment, was the starting point of an awakening whose impact has never stopped quietly trailing me, leaping out at any moment, as if I had acted under orders, according to a 'superior reason' – perfect and unwavering, glued to my skin and to my soul.

I would never stop in Bar-le-Duc again without lowering my eyes and falling into a silence, the same resigned silence my mother had learned to observe.

The pain caused by these thoughts lingers on, as does everything that remains from that journey, though I didn't begin to learn the lesson until much later. When faced with the unavoidable, my mother indeed fell silent, and her silence that day covered the noise of the train axles grinding for the rest of the journey. We never spoke about Sarah again; not at my sister's house or at any other time. The silence that she shrouded me in is not like the silence one might keep to avoid talking, or condemning; nor is it the silence that we all keep about our inner lives. It is the crueller silence of a resignation that holds us prisoner.

I never told this story to anyone, but its memory pursues me, an image endlessly reawakened. Sarah's death became a passageway that opened on to a bottomless pit inside me; and understanding this gave me the key to a great many enigmas. The fear will stay with me until the end of my life. I swear that the action was unbearable and that I had to force myself to do it, in conditions that were both horrendous and easy. I shiver at the thought: I flung her with full force against the wall. At the very second I felt this strength come to me, she stopped moving, overwhelmed by fear, magnetised by my decision, or perhaps overcome by the tenderness I had for her and that she could still feel.

I came away dumbfounded. The experience revealed to me the secret – that my mother, like everyone else, had grown used to keeping safe in silence: what separates man from other beings is his natural ability to disregard his emotions.

A new era was dawning, and I was in Year Zero; I was going to have to learn how to live without my father. On the way, the heady dreams and illusions of my youth evaporated one by one into thin air. I would need to start afresh, prepare myself for a new beginning that would require other sacrifices, other betrayals.

*

As quickly as possible I had to go and travel the world, get away from the burden of constraints, identify the real moments in life, learn to recognise the importance of the setbacks that mould our consciousness – realities that never shed light on pleasant places – and each time to improvise new homelands in the eyes of my travel companions. Then I unwittingly stumbled across a few pivotal books that made me change course and brought me back to France. I returned there to study, then set off again, this time for Cambodia's temples; the Angkor Conservation Centre became the setting for the first stages of my research on Khmer Buddhism.

On 10 October 1971, in the prime of life, I was arrested in a monastery by militia of the Cambodian guerrilla, sentenced to death, and taken to a camp ('M-13'). My daughter Hélène, who was just under four, was left by the roadside. However, the commander in charge of my torture went to great pains to have me freed after three months. Some time thereafter, he was appointed head of security in Phnom Penh, in charge of interrogating and wiping out thousands of enemies of the revolution. At the end of the hostilities, my former 'liberator' disappeared into the countryside until, one day, he was recognised and identified as the 'butcher of Tuol Sleng (S-21)'[2] and he in turn was arrested. He had not forgotten me and wanted to see me again. Immediately afterwards, I wrote a memoir of my imprisonment at M-13 in the forest under his iron rule. In *The Gate* I recalled and discussed the ambiguous relationship that had brought us together – without worrying for a second that I might be betraying the past by using words overly anchored in the present. My only goal in the book was to describe what a young, thirty-year-old French man remembered living through in an extermination camp and what he perceived of the torturer.

I was able to exchange messages with him, and then to see him in prison. I sent him my book. During this time, the machinery of criminal prosecution was set in motion to judge the conspiracy of the Khmer Rouge before a court of international law: the torturer was charged with crimes against humanity and with war crimes.

I now feel a compelling need to go back to my encounter with Duch: it dealt a brutal and premature blow, and inflicted upon me an extreme existential, psychological and emotional shock; I have never stopped feeling the after-effects, spaced out and growing over time – 1971, 1988, 1999, 2009 – like tests that I had to pass to emerge from the shadows towards a new awareness.

These dates on their own won't mean anything to the reader, but they make up an indivisible pattern for me. As they unfold, I see a sequence of sketches that trace out an odd and tragic, phantasmagorical composite drawing, but my mental reflexes prevent me from recognising the face behind it. Sometimes I can decipher it in fits and starts, like a bout of fever that allows a child to grow, when it doesn't kill it. The shock was such that, every time I had to disinter the past, some of my memories arose in such a way as to make me doubt I had ever had them, while others rocked me with the full force of the present, like a boat breaking free from its moorings.

*

1971

Had it been only my detention at the M-13 camp, I would have been left with the impression of simply having had to overcome a personal battle; a battle without any real enemy, I alone facing myself. While imprisoned, my sole obsession was not to miss any signs that might have been a forewarning of my death, like movements in water foretelling an incoming yet still invisible tidal wave. I would have emerged wounded and guilty from the experience, but so relieved that the euphoria I felt at the time of my liberation would have swept everything away, even down to the face and name of the former maths teacher to whom I owed my life. Then and there, I sincerely believed that this story was behind me, that it was over, and that after the war I would be joyfully reunited with my two companions at M-13 – Lay and Son – and resume my research with them.

1988

It was much later, when I recognised the photo of the Khmer Rouge torturer whose prisoner I had been, that a second wave of awareness radically changed things: it was he who had organised the deaths of thousands of people in the horror of Tuol Sleng. It was as if a film of my detention were playing before my eyes, slightly differently – a film shot in slow motion, image by image, as the precise memory of my old fellow detainees at M-13 came back to me in flashes, in the gazes of all the victims whose photos were pinned to the walls of this other detention camp.

As if in a dream, the image of 'Duch' – I had indeed forgotten his name – appeared to me again too, but this time I saw more than ever the duality that defined him – his face sometimes laughing and open, sometimes hermetic and cold – already disembodied, in a dichotomy that he himself was not able to grasp. 'No man . . . can wear one face to himself, and another to the multitude, without finally getting bewildered as to which may be true.'[3] There remained no doubt about this after Tuol Sleng. I let myself once again slip with him into the hollow of that 'grey zone'[4] which both separated and bound us to M-13 – that place of paradoxes where I had been given the opportunity to understand him and to be terrified. Now his nauseating spectre was approaching me, dressed in faded rags held together with shreds of cloth. The rumbling of his voice turned into a shrill moan, which sounded to me like the echo chamber for all human lamentations. I had never heard anything like it: the immensity of his misery stifled any shadow of pity in me. I immediately fled from Tuol Sleng, while meditating on the meaning of things I had seen the seeds of, without recognising them.

And while my memories were recrystallising, I realised that this vision would never again leave me, that I would have to live with it for ever.

1999

When Duch reappeared alive, I got caught again with the same hook, but in a more insidious – though equally tragic – way. Two journalists had found him and immediately recognised him from old photos.[5] The former revolutionary denied nothing, delivered a frank account of his role in the executions, and told of his recent conversion to Christianity. It was no surprise to him: God being in everything we didn't understand, and in everything we didn't want to do, the only explanation for his crimes had to be his own guilt. The time of reprisals had thus begun. Shortly thereafter, I received in Bangkok the tape recording of his first set of recollections, in which he admitted his share of responsibility for the death of 'about forty thousand people'.

In truth, he was no longer part of my thoughts: his self had been overwhelmed, absorbed by the magnitude of his role and actions. The trap, prepared long ago, closed down on me like the magnetic pieces of a Chinese puzzle, silently and with the power of a jaw snapping shut. I saw the elements of the infernal puzzle arranging themselves in my head: although he'd shown me some other part of himself, Duch's biography was reduced to that of the 'Tuol Sleng torturer'.

I could no longer remain silent: the revolutionary individual, the committed 'specialist', the unmasked man, the demanding and moral being, every face of the man I knew jarred with the others, and yet they were to be taken as a whole. His meta-morphoses assumed the gravitas of those ancient tragedies that explain nothing, whose meaning is obscure, but whose sole theme remains the portrayal of life forces, with man struggling in the heart of danger.

I set out to write in haste. I had noted very little during my time in M-13, so my account would be nothing more than a shaping of fragile memories; however, our feelings change colour and blur at such speed that even an immediate and rudimentary capturing of what we have lived through is enigmatic in its own right. An author needs some distance from his subject.

The hardest thing was to go back over my doubts; the most wonderful to sometimes rediscover the freshness of a given moment – turning and re-turning it inside myself, like blood going back through my veins.

2009

On the eve of testifying at the Khmer Rouge trial, I wanted to return one last time to Tuol Sleng. Even after numerous visits, the place fills you with fear.

In the corridors of the former high school, the monster before whom I would soon testify still seemed so present that I was oddly reminded of Joseph Kessel's accounts of the Nuremberg Trials, in which the famed French writer and adventurer displayed all of his talent and his personal disgust.[6] Kessel's descriptions bear the precision of a caricaturist (and with extensive recourse to a kind of anthropometry), and he uses binoculars to magnify the animal nature and degeneration of the features of each of the Nazis crowded together in the courtroom, so that no human being worthy of the name could ever recognise themselves, even the tiniest bit, in these 'false demigods': *enormous face, bald skull, narrow forehead, furtive eyes, flat face, pointy nose, thin lips, treacherous voice, absent chin, soft neck, fat shoulders, round back . . .'*[7]

The point of view depicted here, in Nuremberg or elsewhere – the same point of view man always uses to describe his most detested enemies – remains, despite Kessel's particular talent, that of the majority of court reporters and observers of the period. But my own enemy, alas, would not appear in the courtroom in this light! Since M-13, my target has shifted position. It is more difficult to recognise, though easier to identify: it bears the strange and familiar face of each and every one of us.

The French editor of the confessions of Rudolf Hoess, the former commandant of Auschwitz, went to the trouble of adding an endnote for the reader:

'Hoess's autobiography presents such a considerable historic, 'exemplary' interest, that it warranted publication in several languages. His private life is pertinent to the reader only to the extent that it sheds light on the 'historic' behaviour of the character. Thus [the publishers] do not deem it appropriate to publish Hoess's farewell letters to his family'.[8]

The editor's note refers to the end of Hoess's narrative, when, before he was hanged, he seemed to have found, in certain passages of a more private nature, material not only to reassure himself, but also to show himself in a more complete light, and as such far more monstrous in his duality: 'When this account is used, I would prefer that the passages regarding my wife, my family, my emotional expressions, and my secret doubts not be made public'.[9]

My view is that, on the contrary, the private life of a Nazi officer belongs to us in every way: it sheds light on what we have in common with him. Our similarities are even so terrifying that it should give rise to an emergency measure, if not a new law. What is presented under the cloak of decency (is it the Nazi's private life that is protected here? Or the public's outrage at finding out that he's 'just like the rest of us'?) seems to me just an attempt at confusing matters, a make-believe game that keeps our moral clichés alive. By sticking to a caricature of the great murderers, we think we are keeping them at a safe distance.

Yes, I am interested in the private lives of these men, in so far as these inform their crime – or, whether, even worse, they don't. Beyond the 'tragic behavioural anomalies' that we attribute to bloodthirsty despots as soon as they are *defeated*, exposed, and stigmatised in history books, it is precisely this shared part of sentient beings – the part that I share with them – which is the cause of all my distress and confusion. When we see more clearly the monstrosity of others, we come, sooner or later, to recognise it within ourselves.

Where can we draw the necessary strength, even for a brief instant, to escape the worst of what we do not want to be? I don't know if it's possible without a profound personal crisis. Should we say we're satisfied with a self-righteous rejection of the only available opportunities to recognise ourselves in others? It is not in systems, but in the depths of our disappointments that a new fruit might germinate, under the scaffold of our great sacrileges: the rape of social consciousness, the outrage to morality, the profanation of the human ideal itself.

Looking at Duch on the stand, in the glaring light of the Extraordinary Chambers of the Courts of Cambodia (ECCC), which falls fully upon me, I want to stand up and ask the judges to dare to allow us to hear about the moments when the Khmer Rouge torturer – suddenly dressed up in the same uniform as the Nazi killer – reveals his sensitivity and his doubts, exposes in broad daylight the fundamental aspects of his humanity; how he was a violent, cowardly, frivolous man; and thus deeply human.

*

I have lost the certainly that things, as soon as they occur, take on a shape that stays unchanged for eternity. What was not true then is often made true by us after the fact. The present changes the past more than the future, each new ordeal crowds in on the previous ones to crush them. As always in such circumstances, I think again about the death of my father, of Sarah . . . My pain is throbbing again, my soul is humbled . . . But doesn't death always complement in this way the memories of those we have loved until their final moments?

I think of my two friends Lay and Son, and the victims of M-13's infernal dance; I think of all those who were my companions, however distant, starving and gaunt but all still young and pretty, killed without love. Their faces remain as present in me as those pinned to the walls of Tuol Sleng. I think also of Duch, who everyone stays away from, even his own children; of his ostracised daughter, suddenly soiled by her father's crimes . . . The hardest way to die is by erasing oneself from the hearts of those we love, so that we no longer live within them.

This past is the ever-present womb in which I am reborn. I endlessly go through the stages of my Cambodian ordeal – the one experience that made me acutely aware of my identity. It opened my eyes to a threatening piece of intimate mathematics: what is inside me equals the worst of what there is in others.

How else can we emerge from our blindness, 'this great blindness about ourselves'?[10]

II.

1971 – The Revolutionary

Many of my opinions have changed, but never the ones I
formed about a revolution that I hated right away because it
wanted to replace everything I loved about Cambodia. Of
course its advocates had no shortage of arguments to win
people over and arouse their passions: their noble adventure
was about opposing the Americans, hastening the unstoppable
uprising of peoples that was shaking the world. Their eyes lost
in a dream, they all seemed to agree that war was part of the
suffering that goes with the metamorphoses of life, but that their
struggle stemmed from a higher cause. In Cambodia as well as
in France (where a few unconditional followers of Mao
swooned at the idea of the glorious Khmer Rouge fighters ready
to sacrifice everything), revolutionaries of all stripes had
abandoned intelligence in exchange for the emotions that set
their hearts beating. People sang of the solitude of the guerrilla
warrior as the lot reserved for a few free men, in resistance to
the old world order where masters and slaves were inevitably
bound to debase one another. Faced with such a future and with
so much glory, how could one imagine, even for an instant, that

the young heroes who were taking to the jungle against 'American imperialism' would one day join the ranks of people forced to hide their shame and pander to their former enemies?

Recruited to study Buddhist traditions, after five years I'd had to flee from the Hanoi troops and the invasion of Angkor. I withdrew to the central provinces of Cambodia, though the Khmer Rouge rebellion had begun to rage there. And despite the turbulence of the time, I still hoped to make more discoveries in this country.

On 10 October 1971, I was captured along with my two Cambodian colleagues, Lay and Son, by a handful of Khmer Rouge who immediately carried us away, like fishermen with a good catch. Posted at intervals on a route that bypassed dwellings, young militiamen took turns escorting me in the rain along little paths riven with water-filled ruts. During the first leg of the walk, a chasm had opened in my mind between the researcher, whose existence I had led until then, and the vision of the man I had become, suddenly guarded like a criminal. I was interrogated at a wretched makeshift court, with all its histrionics, in front of spectators who had been gathered together to applaud behind my back.[1] Soon afterwards, my legs were locked in a giant frame that took up the whole floor of a house, where I was reunited with my two companions, both as distressed as I was.

Half a dozen girls lined up to spit in our faces, disgusted, looking at me with prodigious hatred. Arrogant voices shouted up from downstairs that my clothes should be taken off; then a group of men came up to get me. After a brief discussion, they covered my face with a filthy blindfold and pushed me on to a path cluttered with branches which opened on to rice paddies.

My eyes dwelled on things without seeing them, touching them from afar as if with antennae. The exasperation, violence and anger that had been exploding inside me fell away abruptly, and I forced myself to act as if I had courage: my body, which was in turmoil, experienced everything through my eyes – wide open underneath the blindfold, and I moved forward like a robot, in childish obedience.

A heavy sense of my imminent execution was throbbing through my veins, and the less I grasped of the situation, the more it seemed to progress. I remained in shock, and it became as hard for me to catch my breath as to hope or despair. The moment of death seems to conceal an essential, decisive act. I had already seen the way living beings die, especially animals, already half absent at the very instant the deed is done, unsurprised, as if reaching an expected moment. Would it be different for me? What happens inside us when the blow strikes? The villagers of Angkor slaughtered pigs so cruelly with axes, laughing and shouting, that I had once asked them if they would let me slit the pigs' throats myself, with a precise cut, stroking them first to calm them down. How horrible! The torturer must also come to terms with sacrifice. It could be made more human in so many ways . . . But to what end, if this was the way of the world?

The strong hand that had been guiding my muddy footsteps through the gaps in the embankments let go of me and set me to one side, suddenly standing me there, twenty feet away from a firing squad; the whispered words and the clicking of guns reached my ears.

In that instant, when only the situation itself mattered, I no longer felt injustice; I just had a vague idea of it all, and a fear too that it would hurt, like at the dentist's when I was little, before I was settled into the chair and began screaming. In the same way, I glued my mind to every noise with extreme attention, on the lookout for I don't really know what, but the images that formed escaped my grasp one after the other. I remained standing, truly weighing each second that passed and that I saw fleeing away. I heard nothing but the quick beating of the blood in my temples. Then I let myself become absorbed by the constant whittling away of my thoughts, or, rather, by a thousand rough outlines of thoughts, which paralysed me, immersed as I was in that torpor which follows a crisis. I was half dreaming when other guards made me start walking again, along a wider path heading due north.

The next morning, I crossed into a camp without realising it. The blindfold was removed from my eyes and I saw a dozen people sitting around in complete silence. The place was not large; it comprised only four barracks perched on short pillars, covered with a tangle of palm leaves; it was bounded by a stream and the edges of a poorly defined clearing. There were a few shrubs, some undergrowth and several tall trees: they marked the forbidden perimeter in the heart of a bamboo plantation that a handful of men could easily control. I was shackled to other prisoners stretched out at my feet, their faces invisible in the shadows. These men were lined up on a wood rack like objects stripped of their use and reduced to their bare, already faded presence. Did they want to make my sentence worse or relieve the isolation? The silence of my fellow captives seemed like another prison within the prison.

From that instant, my life hung suspended on the reports that Duch, the camp leader, made every day to his commanders, all of whom had been educated in France and dreamed impatiently, as Duch did, of creating a purified country, one radically free of inequality and poverty. Duch himself was a supporter of Marxist communism; he had a deep, intense concern to see justice established in the world, and he was resolved, if necessary, to sacrifice his life for this goal. The man was young, smiling, and the guards who feared him called him 'Grandfather' Duch. I was thirty years old; he was twenty-seven.

Grandfather Duch harboured few expressions, but each one lent him a different face. He never confronted anyone outwardly as an enemy or as someone devoured by hatred; yet his calm actually made us lower our eyes more quickly. Duch seemed destined to wield power naturally, and did not wish to make himself more formidable than he already was. He took on the duties of his commitment unswervingly, as if they were his own demands on the laws of reason.

In this phase of the war during which the Khmer Rouge and their Vietnamese allies opposed the pro-American government of Lon Nol, the revolutionaries were already politically well organised with a very rigid hierarchical structure. Duch – my intuition increasingly told me – was not a freewheeling local leader; just a link in the chain.

He was caught in a constant ebb and flow of reports to send and orders to execute. He did not always seem to approve of the latter either; but he took refuge in the passivity that is one of the most telling qualities of the perfect soldier.

Despite my excessive protests – I can now see them as such – I immediately behaved like a captive whose simple soul was in a state of grief, for whom freedom meant holding his child in his arms, going into villages, dozing at dawn, having the right to come and go anywhere on a motorbike. I stared at Duch intensely, my eyes filled with desperate attention. His work-table was fairly close to the shed where I was shackled, and he paid me frequent visits: this soon became my only connection to the outside world, the one that allowed me to breathe again. When I felt more wretched, more stricken than usual, he was the one I sought out through the foliage. I would catch a glimpse of him sitting, his hand supporting his head, heavy with thoughts he could not share. The leisure I had to observe him was so great that even today I think I can see him in front of me – that small, thin boy, as if moulded in the low archways of the bamboo trees under which we lived in secrecy, always bent as if under some unknown burden. He was a poorly adapted city-dweller and his body seemed to suffer – in his nerves rather than in his flesh – from the humid cold more than from hunger. He seemed in a state of constant, extreme weariness, on the verge of collapse. And I pondered the fact that giving so much for the good of his fellow men hadn't earned him a more enviable position in life.

At M-13, I never came to drown myself in that vegetative state in which so many prisoners gradually lose their impatience and drift away from what was most vital to them. Yet my isolation remained the opposite to that of the village hermits from whom I wanted to take my inspiration – that everlasting aptitude for finding interest in the passing of hours, mastering the art of stretching time out and erasing its tensions. It could make us mad to live with our eyes set on a horizon clouded by the prospect of a radical tragedy; beyond that, there was the tragedy of every day, that was more real and cut deeper – hunger, cold, solitude – but kept us alive nonetheless. Our daily routine depended on our jailers' goodwill. These guards had been blackmailed into serving the revolution, or had bargained for protection for themselves or their families. Far from their villages, they brought with them their youth, their excesses, their ardour.

Scarcely had they arrived than moral degradation wrecked their teenage existence; meanness was unnecessary, but so were kindness, sensitivity and, quite obviously, a certain degree of instruction, as well as intelligence itself. Theory had it that they should be reformed according to a unique, decisive plan: this fast-track education involved a special kind of exile, made up of discipline, organised rivalry and cruelty. War unmasks the individual, bringing out different sides of him, some striking us as good and others as evil. I was moved to tears by these young men's distinctive mixture of glibness and ferocity. If physical domination hardens a man, it also exposes him to the diabolical play of the forces of decline, and I saw the seeds of corruption grow equally among their different personalities. Many of them were heading, without realising it, to the hell of Tuol Sleng (which did not yet exist), where they would soon be called upon to wield their talent, all the more pitilessly because here, at M-13, they had already betrayed their own conscience. And it was as if the harmony among them in this camp hid something bizarrely natural and inevitable, something that stemmed from an order that both brought them closer together and went beyond them.

All ordinary rules were also put on hold. We found ourselves in a world of extreme reality, in another circle of law, at another level of humanity. Obsessed with what was essential, stripped of everything, day to day survival became our most important goal of all and gave birth to a unique strategy for escaping the risk of despair and sheer madness: eating was number one priority. Our minds were haunted by the poorness of meals and we nurtured a silent, sacred relationship to food. All things considered, knowing that we were meant to die, there was indeed something absolutely divine in this gift – as minimal as it was – that was bestowed on everyone. This malnutrition bent forward the starving prisoners' shoulders, making them feel how without responsibility they were, how useless, yet without relieving them of the weight of living. As for the guards, the mere idea of being able to eat well or eat more gave them a sense of their own power.

Finally, Duch had me chained apart from everyone else, near the entrance of the camp, to the pole of a shabby rice-shed that adjoined a clearing in the undergrowth. The chain was barely irritating at the outset, but I came to resent it as a sign of humiliation, to see it as a symbol, rather than a precaution, so much so that I would sit on it to hide it. The place was barely larger than a pocket handkerchief, but three flowers grew there, sprouting from who knows where. From this spot, which I revisit often in my mind, I could sense a variety of smells, noises, distant warbling, strange insects that flew around the space; set aside in this way, I could organise my thoughts more easily than I would have, had I been crowded with my fellow prisoners. The meaning of these sounds was taking shape in strange musical figures. In the past, the sight of nature, like so many sources of life, had infused in me a renewed strength. Here a ray of light could reveal the richness of the parcel of land around me, and the imminent threat of danger, which I knew to be inexorably mine, would mingle with the pleasure drawn from looking at things with a new benevolence. I now saw their delicate forms to be both constant and strikingly fragile. Strange phenomenon: a slight change in position, a shift of the gaze, a difference of a few degrees, was enough, if not to cause delight (for I was consumed by fear), then at least to let some flicker of hope seep into my heart again. Days like these are master classes in learning; suffering provides an uncalled-for, unexpected understanding. I had just arrived at the camp and still felt like a terrified dog, yet the thick fog that cloaked me in darkness was already melting away before me into a vision of nature that my eyes illuminated like floodlights, reaching deep into the under-growth. Such images are engraved in me: I can still see the beautiful brightness that filtered down from the branches far above; fresh shoots rose up at the forest's edge, their stems entwined together. It is a source of wonder how life insinuates its way through in the very heart of desolation! Why do I have this indelible memory of a young fig tree straightening up on the slope, a fine tangle of small pink roots growing around its base?

Who has not had the chance to see for a fleeting moment, when everything is going wrong, an aura gracing reality, and to feel a desire to float away on the surface of things? I began to look at everything and my gaze suddenly seemed able to break down, reorder, and modify the surroundings of the camp . . . Everything that I saw without further examination, brushed against without being able to touch, observed without recog-nising, brought a surprising soothing of my senses as well as of my very ideas. This optimism may have been superficial, but I somehow avoided sinking into the pessimism lurking inside me. Here I could glimpse beneath the surface that the most appealing part of life was built on the repetition of hours; from the depth of my imprisoned existence surged the miracle of an instant, ideal and perfect . . . Nature sent me wave after wave of stimulation, with touching words that imprinted themselves in my soul; and tiny sparks of an overflowing joy fell upon me. Then I saw it dance, come close, send me new sensations, and I realised that by placing me under its spell, nature meant to urge me to stop thinking, stop crying, and to devote myself only to that which could console me; so as to keep me from fears that were overwhelming, and to open my eyes to the joys of the moment. For the horrible dissonance of the present I was to substitute dawns full of freshness and promise, and, without thinking further, to consent from now on to some kind of arranged marriage. To agree to live with that double life that makes you suspect that there are two beings inside you, as if some wretched peddler had taken possession of you and filled your body with so many needs that you feel you could sell out at any moment . . .

Life turns us away from all that scares us, without taking anything else into account, without discriminating amongst our fears – the fear that fills us with worry from the one that keeps us warm and gives us the strength to live: the fear of love that makes us all quiver. To lose the one I loved – never to hold my daughter Hélène in my arms again and rock her to sleep, no longer to see her eyelids close every night and her lips part . . .

Quickly I stopped hearing the sound of Hélène's sobs rising up. Where was I trying to run to? Would my life become only what I perceived – not what I knew – and my heart be entertained by all that was beautiful? I had never before observed nature at such close range, nor with such patience. But if I were to admire this beauty, like a landscape, through gates, I could not accept that they should be the bars of a prison. Immediately I broke with the deception of its appeal, shaken by the idea that in this world below, even suffering could come to an end.

*

Once the tensions had lessened, Duch came to exchange a few words with me in the middle of the day. At first, I dammed up my words, refusing to turn them into sentences, as if I had to sound him out instinctively, the way animals sniff out humans and guess their intentions. Close up, without any particular expression, his features themselves could instil fear. I was yet to learn that these were the features of a man who lived between demons and corpses; the former pushing him to action, the latter to oblivion.

As if to back up the truth of my statements, especially about my research activities, and at the same time to disown the contacts I was suspected of having in Saigon with CIA and KGB agents, I wrote several 'declarations of innocence' and, with his consent, filled the pages of a school notebook that is still with me: childhood memories, drawings, poems, observations on Buddhism, mantras, my curriculum vitae. Nothing else: no daily notes, no information, except what I wrote in Khmer characters on the last day, when it occurred to me to have books and medicine sent to Duch, and I noted down the letters of his name backwards, in an indecipherable form, so as not to forget it. Today, if I happen to open this notebook, its pages yellowed by time, I instantly feel the strange kind of apprehension and physical exhaustion that has kept me from rereading it since.

Duch insisted that what mattered was the declaration of innocence: 'If you're innocent, you must say so! Write it down. Write your biography.' Was it so simple? Duch seemed convinced that it was and I found this disturbing at first. It was like looking out of a window with a view of the bottom of something that I was not allowed to decipher. It came to seem foolish: what faith could be placed in this kind of document when you could put in anything you wanted, without having to provide any proof?

I revised this hasty judgement; recognised the illusion, but not until many years later. These days, I can only laugh at my self-assurance. I have come to accept a deeper truth: all societies assign to their members the terms of their biographies . . . The truth of facts uselessly bares the individual, whereas a fair and thought-through construction along established lines leaves each of us the freedom to create our own self-image and show our good credentials.

This was the unspoken rule among the Khmer Rouge: nobody should reveal anything whatsoever about themselves, or tell their personal story in any way other than as was expected of them. In such circumstances, declarations both of innocence and of guilt were matched outlining an appropriate proclamation of what any individual had the right to reveal of himself. It followed that the torturer would systematically step in, with the mission of obtaining (contrary to what I had naively believed) confessions that needn't so much be authentic as be in compliance with the correct model.[2]

Since the crimes attributed to me existed only in the minds of my accusers, violence imposed itself as the only way for them to confirm their suspicions. In this situation, I had no alternative other than to turn to my interrogator and listen to the suggestions he would give me while going about his business, following the expectations of a questionnaire drawn up by the upper echelons known as the 'Angkar'.[3] That way I would be led to unearth precise and coherent 'memories' that would be perfectly adjusted to predetermined accusations – and that I myself, in an ultimate and calming upsurge, would end up believing.

The leaders' fury did not stop with the fabrication of enemy confessions. After 1975, their exertions would turn towards the autobiographical accounts of the revolutionaries themselves (the newly self-righteous) – an exercise that would become a national practice for hundreds of thousands of people. To be valid, all these biographies, modelled on confessions, had to correspond to certain tactical requirements that were constantly adapted according to the needs of the moment. Indeed, Pol Pot would declare that 'life stories must be good and conform to our requirements'.[4]

Yet Duch's tone towards me remained neutral during my interrogations. Despite his relative youth, he had a quick grasp of the subterfuges that all men use. He gave the impression of someone who has explored the most dangerous areas of life, those parts where you must never at any time let the enemy impose their law upon you. His personal struggle still followed paths that were sheltered from the ordinary mechanisms of violence. Duch never came to me in the guise of an adversary. Sometimes I was even touched by his gaze, half serious and half painful – though every weakness was kept in check. His firm yet scarcely audible voice dissected words, but what he said was never curt or peremptory. He seemed to take advantage of these regular occasions to look at me through narrowed eyes, as if to get a clearer view of his thoughts and the progress of my own. In moves that were always subtle, well thought out and difficult to parry, the man only ever seemed to move insignificant pawns. I got the impression that he slipped gently into everything I asserted in order to see right through me, and then, without missing a beat, that he decoded the information I usually gave in a somewhat confused manner into clearly elaborate ideas of his own. Duch proceeded by watertight deductions, with the calm of scientific procedure, advancing to the truth only if he had distinguished it from fallacy, and often only after having assured himself of my consent; he never returned to the subject thereafter. At first this gave a reassuring impression, but one that soon became terrifying, since this course of interrogation was also likely to lead straight to somewhere. Where exactly? Neither of us pretended to ignore it.

In this way, his task was less to shed light on me and uncover my plans than to make a final decision on my autobiography – as an innocent or guilty one.

Although he was annoyed by my constant rebuffs, the young leader never lost his calm and, technically speaking, maintained his position as inquisitor. I could be sure that whatever I said would be rapidly dissected and weighed as a symptom of my duplicity, my supposed talents as a spy. As far as 'Angkar' was concerned, my only acceptable answers would have had to involve a confession. Under these conditions, it seemed to me a miracle that Duch invariably kept a measure of moderation in his treatment of me, though I also saw this as demonic. Seeing him in this way, I understood that his involvement in the revolution had become part of his entire personality; this commitment was his version of a resistance that he wanted to display in broad daylight – not just for the benefit of his own people, without ever calling upon his interior moral values – in that race to the abyss where men flounder, who have found the courage to survive because they lack the courage to let themselves die. And the terrible thing for those who chose to live was that each and every one was finally condemned to fight alone; the sought-for freedom could not be found in any of the ideals they had embraced.

At the same time, I did feel that Duch progressively wanted to grow closer to me. He circled round the strange, transplanted individual that I was in his eyes. Perhaps that was the reason for the intensive treatment that was applied to me, the meticulous examination of my declarations, the investigations into my leanings, my interests, my precedents – all of it tallied up against supposed sources of information, to which he would make glancing references. For me, in any case, these investigations were the only alternative that gave me any hope; so much so that if he had wanted to break me, the most diabolical manoeuvre he could have used would have been to threaten to deprive me of interrogations.

Duch didn't show me any hostility. Perhaps when one digs inside someone else, that other person quickly becomes familiar; we learn their history, bit by bit, including many things that give us a vague knowledge, but nothing like what is needed to break into their secrets. That is why he remained completely reserved. And no doubt it was his reserve at every instant that made me feel the fundamental gap between us: one that might not be apparent in gestures or expressions, but that was nonetheless radical. Here intuition was needed more than intelligence; there was something impossible to define in him, a sort of remoteness that I could relate to. And I found it extraordinary that I never felt I was 'his' victim. Occasinally it seemed both wonderful and sublime to me that this young 'specialist', while acting with such strong will against imperialism and colonialism, could remain conciliatory towards me (despite all that I represented). I imagined that I had been handed over to him and that his personal responsibility had no place in this arbitrary decision; the question of my release was not at stake for him. Sometimes I imagined that there was the same dispassionate and motiveless relationship between us as between two antonyms. Unlike the other prisoners, methodically perceived as personal enemies of the revolution, the discrimination between Duch and me did not stem from a natural opposition. In a way, I felt that in this conflict which had placed a wall between us I was also on his side, because of our authenticity, because of the frankness with which we each refused to stray away from our own opinions. And although I was forced to note that in him the moral element no longer existed in the same way as it did in me, I observed that he was ready to go back on all his suspicions, but not to disavow a single one of his convictions.

I also think that from the depths of his jungle, Duch, as well as his leaders, underestimated the resemblance of the American forces to Goliath; this perhaps made him a little more conciliatory. So the discussions that arose between us sometimes became quite unusual – and I would counter his arguments, which to my ears had the familiar droning quality of the tunes sung by the French communists. Duch wanted to act for the sake of humanity. His reasoning pompously glorified the Angkar, while the expectation of some worldwide social catastrophe invaded his mind and frightened him much more than the real miseries of the Khmer hinterland, which had been the source of his initial rebellion. What was happening around him horrified him less than the vision of a future annihilation, whose coming he imagined in a space suddenly devoid of humans and filled solely with soldiers from elsewhere – and this sort of imagining shone upon his countenance with a fascinating terror. Facing him, I became a spectator of this immemorial war; I saw the immortal fabric of the sense and nonsense of history unfurl in his eyes, like the underside of the great tapestry that masks the truth about men from us.

Eventually, through the dialogue that had developed, and the rather lively exchanges we had about religion, education and politics – it's true that, with regard to ideology, we were often happy to return to the same commonplace ideas – Duch ended up convinced of my 'innocence'. This conviction, corroborated by the testimony of my two colleagues and the confirmation of what I asserted by sources that reached him from the villages of Angkor, became the source of a conflict between him and Ta Mok, the local leader.

Since every prisoner had to be eliminated after his confession, the whole plan had always been to quickly establish the time of my execution. However, faced with the inconsistency of the accusations that had been made against me, and perhaps too because a sort of friendly interest had grown between us, Duch had not been able to bring himself to comply with the orders, or to let something be carried out that he felt was unjust. The affair was referred all the way up to the Permanent Central Committee, which was headed by a certain Saloth Sar, the future Pol Pot. Ta Mok's recommendations were not followed. Against all the odds, I was released.[5]

As he escorted me on my way back to freedom, the brother-hood that briefly brought us together during the last hours of my detention imprinted on my memory a deep sincerity and gravity that few people experience, unless they're ready to run the same risks. It was like an unnatural pact, secretly sealed amid struggle and fear. I was now free, and I knew that my fate was more enviable than his. Before we took leave of each other, in a moment's silence, I felt I related to him better than through all the words we had already said. Afterwards, he went back to the other prisoners my former co-detainees to continue his work, with no other prospect than to be dragged into the same catastrophe. I had a vision of one of those carnivorous fish that inhabit rivers, which you spot lashing about in the middle of a shoal of their prey, as the still distant rim of a fishing net starts closing in on them all.

*

It may seem hard to believe: to have endured seventy-seven days of crushing fear (fear of being executed with the blow of a spade and leaving Hélène alone), coupled with a feeling of guilt made worse by paranoia, and then to emerge from that unharmed. I mean devoid of any real thoughts about what I had undergone. Nothing but weak impressions, a few reflections; no deep-reaching personal investigations – aside from the notion that I had been the victim of a stupid accident, whose consequences might have blighted my life by putting an end to my research at the local branch of the French School of Asian Studies (EFEO). But for the future, no repercussions to fear, no backlash, and no strings attached that might be liable some day to pull me back.

I remember, though, the mass of thoughts that moved me. What I could perceive, I felt not as an event of limited impact, but as symptoms or premises of something of a greater magnitude, which seemed already to have made its mark on my life, whose significance went far beyond its intrinsic importance and seeming extent, but which was so incomplete that it would never see the light of day.

The memory of a French planter from South Vietnam (Jean Delhomme) came to me. He had been forcefully dragged away by the *bo doi* [soldiers], tied up and blindfolded for twenty-one days. I had met him soon thereafter. I lowered my eyes upon hearing of the ordeal he had been through, imagining him as a tower of strength, rich with mysteries and initiations, compared to which my own imprisonment had left me untouched. My own ordeal concealed no glory, no revelation, and my release was stained with the shame of returning without my two companions. At the time, victims were not warned about possible trauma – not to protect them from it, but to lessen its violence. And in fact, the shock didn't really hit me until thirty years later when I learned that Lay and Son had been executed. What is the weight of so many other victims when compared with the death of two friends, the guilt of which saddles you for life?

Son, the younger of the two, was a tactful, friendly, talented boy, whom I had hired at the Silver Pagoda in Phnom Penh because he drew well; and I was very fond of Lay, whom I had met as soon as I'd arrived in Cambodia. Disoriented by so many novel, strange ways of living, I had relied on him when I took my first steps far into villages, and also when I tried out my temperament, my ways of thinking, my habits as a young Frenchman, to see what sort of useful things I could draw from this new world. My life was beginning; we were the same age, and through him, I could try out unlikely propositions as if in a game from which I always saw myself emerging with my head high, like one of those hardened peasants I so wanted to get close to. When we spoke together, I said loud and clear that there were some things I would never do . . .

But, at the heart of the Cardamom forest, trying to ensure the liberation of my two friends as well as my own simply by refusing to leave without them would have been a rather presumptuous poker move. Weighing my chances, Duch made this clear to me in no uncertain terms. The risk was putting at risk my own release by placing the affair once again in Ta Mok's hands. If I was allowed to go free, it was because I was a foreigner. The revolution needed Lay and Son to remain where they belonged, in the maquis. I would rather have been beaten, to avoid having to make the choice to leave on my own, unable to bluff any longer at a game where I was fooling no one but myself. So after sitting for a while next to them, I left alone, with no further ado – every bit the coward, the feeble individual that the news of my liberation had made me. As it had been with Sarah, their freedom put my own in jeopardy; and in this ghastly exchange, my life became more important than theirs. I hate this moment in my existence without which I might have lived serenely, with enough aplomb to dare to judge others. After we said goodbye, and I finally waved from afar, the view I offered of myself had become so pitiful that for an instant I really wanted to believe – as they themselves were convinced without saying so – that behind the facade of my liberation, this departure would indeed be my last journey, and that it was my turn to walk towards an imminent death . . .

In that rudderless sense of time to which the Khmer Rouge had sent me back, in that space where nothing happened, where death was so close that everyone kept it in mind when the slightest decisions were needed – whether it was still worthwhile to lance a boil, for example – I had lived as if in a secret society, with its punishments, its mysteries, its rules. The penitent learned the lessons of silence – that deadly silence I had felt afflicted with since adolescence, which I now met again with an atrocious aftertaste of déjà-vu.

As for Duch, it became hard for me to talk about him. I even think that, immediately after my release, the man had already ceased to exist for me – or rather, did not yet exist, except as a cog among other cogs I had encountered in a world of robots, from which he could not escape. But about the man himself, nothing at all! About his personality, his contradictions, his yearnings and his dreams, nothing more than about my friends the hens, the haunting stench of the forest shit holes, the young guards to whom I had to report, the mortification of being chained, my beloved post, my sobs, the tarantula, the little girl under my protection, the sparks of heat flashing up in the air, my dangerous outbursts of impatience, the hunger that rallies the spirit, the piercing chirping of the oriole, the erection that woke me from sleep, the *chhlik* tree and its white trunk, the stormy nights through the thick of the bamboos, my fits of anger, the impromptu visits of little bats at nightfall, the distant noise of a truck, the indifference of planes, the guards' barracks, my surges of anxiety, the torments of despair that infected everything so that I could find nothing to soothe it, and that sudden dire fright – from which I will never recover – when I found out that the person who strove so hard to save me was also the one who exerted himself to beat others – nothing . . . Nothing about that either . . . Nothing!

*

On the eve of my release, as he was now no longer entirely forced to keep silent with me, Duch began speaking with less caution, the way you finally open up to someone you'll never see again, about a question that is perhaps so important that you've never spoken about it to anyone. Duch agreed to explain things to me coldly, but sincerely, without holding back, without resentment of anyone, talking about a task that needs to be done properly, as if he were saying, with a wave of his hand: 'Well yes, what do you expect, that's obviously what I have to do . . .' Finally the young commander with whom I spoke every day – upon whom my life depended, and whom I tried to understand by watching at length – had revealed that he had to beat the prisoners himself.

But confessions change depending on who is hearing them. For him, torturing was part of a whole. It was nothing more than putting the ardour of his commitment into practice, the action being in proportion to the greatness of the revolutionary ends. This was the price of victory over imperialism. This he told me in few words, without making one thing seem to be another, without denying, in his own words, the horror of a task that he could only carry out by making himself literally 'out of breath'.

Thirty-eight years later, summoned by judges to shed light on his statement to me about this suffering inflicted upon the prisoners,[6] Duch remembered that the first time he attempted to hit one, he had had to stop, overcome by vomiting, too exhausted by his own effort in the action.

I had written about the episode with no moral aim: on 24 December 1971, I was at the M-13 camp and something happened, at nightfall, that made my blood freeze. In this respect, the young leader had become my elder, and I admit that it took quite an effort for me to get used to seeing him in this light.

The idea that he too could be a killer had occurred to me several times, but just as quickly it seemed to make no sense. On each occasion when he might have revealed himself as such with me, what I could see in him persuaded me of the opposite. The tasks he had taken on in the service of the revolution – as a major link in the chain that bound each prisoner to Angkar – seemed to require him only to devote his intelligence and skill to the art of summarising and writing reports. Inflicting violence upon prisoners was not his domain.

But near the fire that crackled before us that night, as the thought of my imminent liberation was seeping into me, the words that emerged from his mouth, like the keys to a coded enigma, directed me towards a new understanding. I remember the fragility in his voice as he varied it to alternate his shouts with those of his prey. The man wanted to bring his victims' pain to life, so that I could better measure his own. All my disgust was focused on his 'sacrifice', as if it were something I had felt already. Between the embers of the fire and the flames that burnt before us, heat had suppressed any kind of dividing line and brought us closer. That Christmas Eve, the whole sky fell upon my head. I found myself presented with a torturer's kit that fitted me like a glove. I knew myself to be capable of the worst deeds; but the awareness of my crimes remained buried – it wasn't *me*, just an image, a reflection. And yet, hadn't I already decided, during those weeks when I didn't know his intentions, to escape the camp and to stone anyone to death – even a child – who might get in my way?

Those few seconds shattered the space that separated me from the innermost part of myself, a sudden denouement in which I understood that to be 'human' was not a quality that belonged to some, and not to others. Any man was my brother, even down in the abyss. 'The Permanence of Man'[7] appeared to me now in the worst of everything that was done on the surface of earth; and the question raised was finally about the nature of the archetype reproduced each time.

It's obvious that I was the only one to whom Duch could say these things, possibly to try out his honesty without risk, but also to challenge me when he saw that I believed, so naively, that violence was only the choice of brutes. It's a fact that his subordinate fitted this profile: a big bear of a man named Soum,[8] who was stubborn and impervious to the feelings of others, whose obtuse intelligence was united with brutality. Faced with my ignorance, the young torturer chose to provoke me, in a manner that was both so forthright and guileless, and yet so utterly violent, that I could have torn out my hair in despair at the idea that in his place I might have done the same.

The secret of his confession was probably known to all but me; yet it seemed bordering on the insane that he should speak up. I accepted it as a proof of confidence. Though such frankness – from a man who had gone so far astray that he was able to admit it himself, and even tell me about it – was the final step towards my utter unsettling. We sat there in silence, in the smoke from the bonfire – the crackling of its last embers unable to cover the sounds of the glowing night. Duch had this particular expression, a seriousness that was specific to him – his gaze so different from that of others – and which then gave me a whole new idea of what was singular about him: the presence of a secret that did not allow him to see men the way I could see them. His words were terrifying, and delivered so directly, in the way one might affirm the inevitability of a law or the obviousness of an injustice. They echoed off a deeper distress within me, all the more so as the meaning of his confession sounded intimately close to me: life forced us to a juggling game of ups and downs; the same man had to chase away remorse from his soul, where lived, side by side, selfishness and generosity, idealism and cynicism, honesty and deceitfulness, cruelty and sensitivity, the other's death and one's own – staying constantly between two dangers in which each tried to surpass the other. Facing Duch, my mind was confronted with a task, as if before a combination lock. The strange thing being that, having dealt with it so little, it seemed proportionally simpler; I quickly sensed that it was my own heart, myself, that it was me that I was trying to open – that the enigma he presented was the echo of the one inside me.

This instant revealed us to ourselves and to the other, as if there could be no knowledge of self except through mutual recognition. I entered into such an atrocious resonance with him, coupled with such a feeling of identification, of belonging, of reciprocal danger and shared responsibility, that I wondered if I wasn't running a risk by not calling for help, if I weren't slipping into a sort of complicity by saying nothing, by not getting up, by not appearing to condemn actions that I suddenly feared could as easily have been my own.

*

Back in Phnom Penh, once I had been reunited with my daughter Hélène and my family and was feeling a happiness that is still within me, it did occur to me that this story might leave traces, but I no longer spoke of all that. To tell the truth my first concern was the risk I faced of being sent back to France. I would have been distraught to have to leave Cambodia. And, as expected, this was what the curator of Angkor had planned: 'There's nothing more here for you'.

I wrote to Jean Filiozat, the head of EFEO in Paris, to report what had happened. I explained that in my jailers' hands I had changed the subject of my research on Buddhism and had decided to devote myself to texts in Khmer. I asked him to maintain his trust in me. The director immediately sent me a brief message saying that he had arranged for my leave of absence – 'The paperwork has been done.' For the first time I had the feeling of existing inside the School, of being one of its members in my own right, of belonging to that family of special people whom I so admired. Forget the war and the Khmer Rouge, that day was one of the best in my life!

Still, beyond assurances from the French, the risk of Phnom Penh's governmental soldiers taking revenge could not be ruled out. They were free to decide to have me expelled, as retaliation against the French government for favouring the revolutionaries, or under the pretence that I'd cosied up to the Communists in exchange for my liberation. Afraid of finding myself once again suspected of espionage, I had insisted on translating for myself some documents that the guerrillas had asked me to give to the French – working as carefully as a cat burglar and refusing to trust the discretion of the Cambodian interpreters paid for by the embassy.

On a personal level, there were no after-effects once my detention was over. Without any trouble, I talked about what had happened both to those close to me and to the chargé d'affaires and the military authorities. A high-ranking officer of Lon Nol's cabinet had even insisted on questioning me himself, with much care, in the presence of the consul. It was just that when describing certain things, or lingering over some detail or minor remembrance, I could talk effortlessly about what I had seen, but was unable to reveal anything personal. A kind of inhibition of my thoughts seemed to filter everything deep inside me. In this way, and after barely a few weeks, it was as if I had lost all memory of the humiliations and of the shame I had endured – even Duch's very name. I felt bound to him; I owed it to him that I had returned and was alive; and I was aware of this. There was much more to it all, but I could not see how to explain it, how I might come clean and disclose what seemed by its nature so hidden, or so confused, without losing my way in endless meanderings that I would not have the strength to follow to the end. I felt exhaustion in advance just at the thought of it. Deep within, the memory of Duch filled me with a radical fear that I could neither explain nor communicate.

*

My move to Cambodia had primarily stemmed from a kind of unsociability mixed with a very keen desire for a change of environment, as if happiness had to come from a far-off country. This journey reflected my state of mind, the way I looked ahead, after my father's death: to get under way, to head in one direction as far as possible, even if my self-confidence had been chipped away.

At the same time, I felt that my ambition to carry out research was governed by an intense, new-found need to write: not just as an ethnographer, using objective capacities, making notes, recording facts; instead it would be writing that comes from within and that I could perceive, more and more, as giving shape to our thoughts. In the village, I had immediately distinguished between these two regions of ourselves – one material, the other spiritual – while the two spheres were more rarely separate for the researcher. Both elements were formed in a shared mindset and with expectations that complemented each other on different levels – here a first clue to a hypothesis, there an unexpected word or image that changes the way one looks at things, their correspondences unveiled. Until then I'd believed that one had to think beforehand in order to write. It suddenly became clear that I had to write first to begin to think, as if our knowledge of ourselves slowly drifts along as we are writing.

For me, writing became a work of creating mosaics, which was also close to my research and excursions in the field; the real difficulty lay in striking the right balance between what I managed to see and what I could render in words – to rush headlong, at the first intuition, to instinctively look, listen, feel, and in the end to arrive at something quite remote from what I originally expected, but perhaps more attuned to what I would think thereafter. Writing aroused questions, challenged presumptions, brought me closer to myself by moving away, to this ideal space where my observations could unfold between gaze, language and writing.

Along the way, I discovered the wonderful, unexpected world of intersubjectivity: a 'secret agent'[9] was there, who never left me, but whom I instantly addressed as if it were another. We never write alone; we write in the shadow of some stowaway who expresses himself for us, speaks in our ear, becomes our interpreter, and who brings us to hear what we want to say. With him as an escort, I started upon uncertain paths, including the most adventurous, aware that a maze of complications would defeat my reasoning but urged on by the idea that 'you can never go as far as when you no longer know where you are going'.[10]

Strange thing, this stubbornness. This effort carries a secret value, so true is it that the goal you assign yourself is rarely the one you reach. Within us, the man at rest and the man in motion are dissimilar beings.

Everyone wants to follow their own rules, to appear authentic, with the uniform they have been given; but life is there, carrying its load of occasions, of injunctions, its imperceptible pulse dragging along the good and bad. What we call 'life' is the sum of surprises that become carved on our flesh in indelible marks, at uneven intervals and in indistinct moments.

*

When I arrived at the Angkor Conservation centre, everything was so new to me that I had the impression of moving towards strange, hard-to-imagine events. I could not wait to leave my housing at the back of the French campus. As I dreamed of other ways of life – of discovering a world where I would lose my bearings, free from any kind of bonds – I received in the Cambodian countryside the gift of a space without limits; its grandiose perspectives I wanted to make my own.

I alone was confident that I would be able to adjust to this existence, and I bowed without restraint to the need to establish immediate parallels, to blend in with people so as to better resemble them, to form relationships without any interpreter, the way travellers proceed, laughing together. One expresses feelings, one tells a story – then the story of one's whole life – time goes by and everyone calmly goes on their way, pleased with this little nothing, but feeling as if they have a better self-understanding. Years later my propensity to imitate the next man saved me in the Cardamom hills.

In Cambodia, I felt remote from the formalism that was in full swing in France. The 1970s was an era of all-encompassing systems; structuralism had imposed itself as the safest path to the truth. But the question of the personal involvement of the researcher, who risked putting his own subjectivity into play, did not arise for me. I felt capable of only one thing: living to the fullest with all my emotions, my values, my sense of things, without trying to take any stance in relation to an 'object of study', and without seeking to emerge intact from my observations. If I wanted to understand what my fellow human was like, I could not avoid being affected and challenged by him. My quest was based on an intimate approach to others, which called into question my beliefs and desire for knowledge; it forced me to abandon the 'bird's eye view' in favour of the meaning that emerges on the ground: the types of trees, the songs of birds, the distinctiveness of the Cambodian cart, the mystery of the holy texts.

As for the Nancy native that I never stopped being, settling in this land of asylum was a struggle against his mental habits. I am sure this high degree of personal commitment provided me with the keys I needed to understand the many ways in which man could be human, with its whole gamut of nuances, including variations in which the most ordinary feelings, or the most disturbing, could take on precious importance.

It took me a while to achieve my goals, to leave the protected housing compound in the Angkor Conservation Centre, and resettle in Srah Srang, a village located a few miles from Angkor Wat, the site's largest and most renowned temple.

As soon as I arrived in the village, I was asked to attend the cremation rites for an old peasant who had recently died. I was invited, along with the other guests, to ingest a small piece of the deceased's liver – pulled from the fire's ashes and still burning hot – as a token of my familial bond to him. The underlying principle was that it allowed the guests to take part in his ascent to the skies. It was my first chance to adapt to the beliefs, rules and surprising proprieties of the unknown world and its inhabitants to which I had chosen to deport myself.

There was nothing 'natural' about my frame of mind; a next-door neighbour might be completely different, and equally difficult to comprehend . . . Strange to see how the moments of our existence come together, as if all that we live through isn't woven from a single thread. And while I now find it wonderful that chance allowed me to make some of these encounters, I can't stop myself from thinking about Duch, as I would about an extraterrestrial whom I also met on the road.

Our fate enters the stage through hidden doors, and always in a new costume. I wonder how our memory makes its choices as to which characters it distinguishes amid the crowd. How are we to explain the influence these people constantly exercise over us? There must be a special quality in their vital force – that force in them that we feel too, beyond all morality, and which we make out because it is part of our shared heritage.

In my altered circumstances, which were meant to make me the different man I wanted to be, my very first move in the field, and the least thought through, proved most decisive: I got hold of a large collection of ancient manuscripts – stored and recopied for centuries in the countryside – and I quickly started to translate them. The bombardment of villages by the governmental army was destroying the pagodas, and the old monks called on me to record their treasures before everything had been destroyed. Saving the last texts of this literary tradition took on the significance of a personal duty for me, in which I invested myself without calculation.

This monastic labour swallowed up a lot of time throughout my life, but I regard it as the calling that I needed in order to nurture and finesse many an aspect of my discernment. For to translate is to build bridges; it is to project a way of thinking, a language, beyond itself. It is to contort one's mind in an extreme sort of gymnastics, sliding from this way of seeing things to that way, to restore meaning in all its strangeness, careful not to erase anything, or adapt it to our own images; to create in one's self enough space to welcome new things, without trivialising them, without drowning their specific message or reducing them to the limits of one's own language, that is, of the world in which one happened to watch, love, exist until then. Just as a painter gets noticed for his unique way of seeing nature, one language distinguishes itself from another by its style. To compare human languages – to balance appropriate meanings, to transpose into one system what is expressed in another – is to learn to balance accepted terms drawn from a different understanding of life: the task lies in our greater or lesser willingness to revise our own judgement. To do that, you must take a leap, and that leap is not a shift in position; it is a transformation.

If I strove to understand what was going on in the head of the peasant to whom I wanted to relate, I had to understand him not by copying but by translating, banking on the fact that a stranger delivers only an image of what he is willing to say, modified by his hesitations, his presuppositions. I had to allow for the fact that what would be intelligible to me would also be deceptive. Hence, making it so that these distant, unreachable beings – I mean beings from whom so many prohibitions distance us – could confide to me in their language something that I could articulate in my own, through a human, global, sensitive, personal process . . . I had to do all I could to distinguish myself from them as little as possible, but also to overcome myself so as to realign the soul within myself.

*

This daunting challenge, these habits I'd fallen into, this systematic obsession with wanting to see into others and sound them out from within . . . it all turned into a nightmarish operation after I arrived at M-13. For it is one thing to endow someone else with one's own particular experience, and it is another to slip inside his mind and take on his shape, when this shape is intolerable and yet so congruent that one cannot doubt it is also our own. A Khmer Rouge jailer was the opposite of me; but he *was* still me, even in decay.

The empathy that little by little allowed me to understand what Duch was feeling, as if I felt it myself, had to do with the circumstances leading to my liberation. I had seen so much darkness congeal in his withdrawals, his sighs, his hesitations, that the only possible cause for my liberation – the same one that allowed him to summon all his courage and his strength in the camp – had to be his spirit of rationality. And though chained up in front of him, I regarded him as my contemporary, and the words that filtered through my terror said, 'I feel, I share; I make your dread and your fate my own'. I was freeing him from his own fear and was able, without planning it, to hide from him the detestable image ('Do you have no pity?') that his other victims all projected on to him. My face became his own, and that forbade him from killing me.[11]

*

My return to Phnom Penh created quite a stir. I had seen the devil up close dancing in the midst of the fire with his rebel angels; and as a man in the know, just back from the other world, my doubts about a governmental victory over the Khmer rouge boded ill for those who, not liking the Khmer Rouge any more than I did, were betting on their defeat. When it came to talking with my colleagues, even the closest ones, like many French people whose positions on Cambodia and the war in Vietnam were politically so clear-cut, it would have been inappropriate to put my own existential concerns – especially about the events that led to the unforeseen outcome of my capture – into the mix of the situation. As to the leader of

M-13, no compromise was to be considered: the guerrillas were either terrorists or people of uncommon virtue; it was all about which side you were on. It was not in accord with the thinking of the time to avoid such labelling by dichotomy, or to suggest that other dividing lines were possible. No matter the show of humanity that my liberator had displayed, he was still fighting in the cause of a hated revolution, and any sympathy he might inspire could have a dangerously seductive influence that had to be warded off. In any case, in the capital each and every one lived through the experience of the war, over-emphasising their own concerns, with little consideration for the peasants who had no choice but to come to terms with the Khmer Rouge. Everything got muddled. Left with the disgraceful actions of the pro-American governmental troops' recruits and the puzzling imbecility of the pro-Chinese of all stripes, the entire country was sinking into a little more gloominess with every day. Even though the forces on the scene might alter some articles of faith in their case for violence, none would change their methods in the least. It was easy to see that both sides were descending into areas where merit vanished, where only suffering held its own.

In Phnom Penh, memories of the acute aggravation of my senses under the Khmer Rouge's iron rule – that ability to feel from within what went beyond simple understanding – came back to me, and they were in opposition to the intellectual code of my contemporaries. I could no longer reason as they did, nor could I reason as myself. I seemed to lack the freedom to make people hear what my whole being wanted to say, about my own motivations, man's hidden instincts, the other face of the torturer – about all the truths that went against the so-called wisdom of public morality. Whatever part Duch's leniency had played in my release, the psychological mechanisms put in motion, in his conscience as in mine, resonated in ways I did not dare ponder, or even return to, because they put me in a precarious position vis-à-vis my own education. From this journey of paradoxes I was returning with an enigmatic impression of zones full of shadows. Why hadn't I taken an immense dislike to Duch? Had I been his victim, or not? I had confronted him about the truest, most sincere, most authentic things in us, without for a single instant sharing the political commitment for which he was ready to die, and thus to kill. But at the time, as soon as I endeavoured to picture his motives, it seemed possible to understand what he was doing, what he had to do. In those instants, the cruelty of his occupation was nothing more to me than the hopeless reflection of the vilest forms of human behaviours, all issuing from the same original depths.

Some people are like magnifying glasses that allow us to access the great taboo background to which our pupils adjust with such difficulty. What we see then is what is usually wrapped inside everyone's secrets. At M-13, I managed to look into these things fully, and the sudden vision of a Duch quite like other mortals was a call to arms – in a fundamental battle against myself which I now know will never come to an end.

Conditions permitting, a person in danger of death will sympathise with those who threaten him. I had already been threatened, like everyone else, at school or with some of my friends. But there, in that extermination camp, the dubious position of the guard and the condemned man – which 'victimology' popularised later under the term Stockholm syndrome – sent me down whirling inside. The appellation stems from the survival instinct that urges every victim to become attached to the fate of his torturer, sometimes even to defend him, to the point of refusing later on to testify against him. With Duch, I think I went even further: separated from everything, and surprised in my meagre nudity, fear forced me not simply to be 'sympathetic' to him (that would have been pointless), but to improvise multiple scenarios of approach, in order to experience as fully and as sincerely as possible all of his reactions, to capture his attention and make him sensitive to my fate – to 'seduce' him intuitively, in my own way, so as to remain credible, and so that a real feeling of identification could develop between us. My life was at stake, and without taking the risk of cheating – not caring about untangling the conscious from what rose from the subconscious – I placed all my hopes in him, angrily, but with all my heart. For instance, I discreetly manoeuvered him so that he would face the consequences of his actions, finding roundabout paths to make him sense, by exaggerating them, all the intrinsic risks that would ensue from my death: a canonical literature of texts barely uncovered would be lost; ancestral rituals would never be studied; not to mention a child who would be crying somewhere, calling out for her father . . . I now believe that no man can resist this; his mistake was to listen to me, my strength to make myself heard.

Just as Duch had planned not to torture me and to gently extract fuller confessions from me, so I had imagined from a tactical point of view that it was by remaining sincere – to the point of shouting, of open rebellion— that my innocence would be clearest to him. I knew that one mistrusts a person most when they disguise their voice. And at this game, keeping in mind the submissive relationship that Duch entertained with his bosses, I wonder to what extent he himself fell into an equivalent dependence with me, balancing the constraints of his conduct by striving to protect me and refusing to kill me; I see a similar pattern in our behaviour – his in his relation to his hierarchy, and to Ta Mok in particular, mine in my relation to him.

We were both probably partly aware of the situation, but only in an unspoken way, since no one there seemed ever to have enough time to think: in this imprisoned space that we all lived in, and where everyone had his assigned place, no one thought about anything but surviving. But, paradoxically, there came a moment when the obsession with personal safety took a back seat; the need to 'keep going' was so central that there was no room left for thought, nor even fear. At the same time, by triggering that very mechanism, fear acted on everyone, from the killers to the killed. My endeavours to keep Duch on my side – which I exercised over him as much as over the guards who reported everything to him – seemed to be executed in their own, freewheeling style, without operation of the will, from a subconscious hinterland to which I had no access. Thus we lived in invisibility, he and I, in the midst of the others, in a symbiosis that mated us without making us closer to each other, but on which more or less all our behaviour was modelled, my own depending on what I could see of his, and vice versa. I remained alert, involved to an extreme degree, wholly focused on his person, constantly genuinely striving for assimilation.

I imagined him, at the top of his watchtower, caught going about his two lives: the first in broad daylight, the second in the dead of night. And while these two poles of ordinary life combine in our dreams, I wondered which brought him more pain: his efforts at survival in the diurnal existence, or the moral judgement that was taking shape within him during his nocturnal solitude.[12] When he was in my sight, at the thickest of his darkness, I took advantage of his frightening candle to go and bury my face in the maze of my own obscurities. I found deep inside myself so much confusion and contradiction that I wondered whether I would have resisted any better than him the powers of falsity and their corruption, whether I would have been better equipped not to break the laws of morality. I remembered many a minor choice I'd made in my life; was I capable of questioning those choices, once the small circle of people I knew had recognised them as authentic and true?

Never again would I see my fellow man as before. Duch set a storm of questions whirling around my head, the kind we only ever encounter in fairy tales or mythology and that, later in life, we only put to children.

I would have liked to be able to return to the warm shadows of my childhood nights, when I was afraid of the devil and yet lived in some comfort. Since then I've learned that there is always a real monster hidden in the wardrobe.

The horror no longer appeared to me to be the effect of some disease, of a constitutional defect that prevented the 'free development of the soul', the deficiency of dark natures barely touched by the rays of light. I did not know that the orchestration of evil might not exclude sincerity or generosity. I imagined that savagery was a thing innate, the tribute paid to nature by dangerous beings, regardless of causes and conditions. I believed that killing and beating were stains on a character, and stemmed from nature, a need for domination, a deviant psycho-physiological disposition. I didn't know that the human condition, which makes each of us a beloved father, a beloved son, a cherished being, might never protect us from the monsters that lurk within.

Duch had caused the scales to fall so painfully from my eyes that it became impossible for me to measure on my own the consequences of what I had just experienced without beginning to shiver. His mask, which he lifted at times before me as he got to know me better, allowed me to see the invisible: continuity and disruptions made me see him now as a killer, now in his human interiority, like those 'transformation masks' that animists put on, which in Cambodia portray an animal or a human being whose gaping mouth opens on to another face. These masks reveal the inside of a man, as a paradigm of subjectivity, and they also symbolise the tangled world where everyone must go to discover the other. They all generate that repulsion we feel when animals display human characteristics.

III.

1988 – The Torturer

The land of the Khmer became a second spiritual homeland for me, the ever-deepening symbol that stands for all I have learned, and even more unlearned, along with everything about the ancient culture that remains dear to me.

At the mention of those things past which still surround me, what images rise up in my memory? First of all the patchwork landscape of the Cambodian countryside, dotted with uniform borassus palm trees and their aerial globes that stand out like shadow plays. (This image obviously hints at the structure of the world.) Then, Sihanouk's flight, the North Vietnamese invasion, the little kingdom weighed down with chains, Lon Nol's withdrawal, the defeat of the United States, the rise of the Khmer Rouge . . .[1] These events made infinitely more tragic to me the horror that the peasants went through, not to mention the incredible heroism of their sons in this idiotic conflict; where the Khmers, from both sides, had become victims of the ineptitude and indifference of commanders who were obeying the orders of foreign powers. It's not possible to recover from such a defeat. Then, I see the silent fall of the capital, the beginning of the terror, and the arrogance of the victors in imposing their beliefs on the imagination of the masses – no one daring to speak out in public – the finale of a population. Archaic savagery was once again unleashed within the confines of this poor country, and the new ideology only worsened its moral collapse. The Khmer Rouge turned the Cambodian people into a corpse. Their triumph was a milestone in the life of this nation, for it was not just many human lives that were annihilated along the way, but also the heart of the subtle mechanics that govern intimacy . . . For generations to come these things will provide material for terrifying tales that the survivors will tell their bloodless children and their grandchildren.

I can't live in this country any more. Too many places have become taboo; it is as if I had to go back to the slaughterhouses of Nancy, or walk around in a world against which I have no protective shell. Many of these are places where men have taken the gloves off against herds of defenceless people mechanically following collective rules, just as all killers did throughout the vile workplace of slaughterers that was the twentieth century. In Cambodia, a country deprived of change its people could believe in, many still eagerly keep themselves busy hurting the same people all over again and take advantage of the chaos.

Duch, back then – I had all but forgotten about him.

*

After Phnom Penh was taken over by the Khmer Rouge, I found refuge in the French Embassy with all the remaining foreigners,[2] before being evacuated to Thailand on 6 May 1975, to a village in the northeast (Ta Tiyou), not far from the arid zones where the first refugee camps were being set up. Many refugees were fleeing there to hide. They told in detail of what they had seen on their way, with dreadful particulars that no one dared believe.

The shelters dug right in the ground had turned fetid, and were alarmingly overcrowded, with filthy, lice-ridden canvas tarps for roofs; the refugees were exploited by gangs under the control of Thai soldiers. Theft, rape and murder were common. I can still see the people from the French Embassy – a few journalists and humanitarians, all of them sickened by the situation – who asked me to go with them to a less crowded camp farther south. Not far from Trat, right in Thai territory, it had a miserable mix of displaced people, and they had officially come under the administration of the Khmer Rouge! As soon as we passed the gate, the difference was impressive: cleanliness, silence, discipline – it was striking. In the middle of the immense open space we had to cross, we walked by a half-naked boy tied to a post; he had fainted under the scorching sun. How many days had he been there? Disgusted, ready for a run-in, our group asked me to find out what it was about. A supervisor who had come to meet us replied in a friendly way that a measure of discipline could not, unfortunately, be avoided; this was the fate reserved for thieves. The kid had been caught with his hand in one of the bags of rice allocated to the collective. Caught off guard by an explanation that went against their own sensitivities, my companions, uncomfortable, were unable to utter any protest, so favourably did the order that reigned over the camp of the Khmer Rouge contrast with the wretchedness in which the other camps were wallowing, and which they fiercely condemned. They coyly praised the

foreign people undergo such treatment, instead of perpetrating it on their blood brothers. This was also the bad luck of the Khmers, since the argument of a 'fratricidal war' gave grounds for the non-intervention of the entire West. The 1975 'peasant revolution' was a monumental hoax orchestrated on the provocation of foreign (Chinese, North Vietnamese) advisors who knew how to use all the local resources to exploit the old Cambodian ideological divisions – between city and country – and take advantage of the most recent layer of Western guilt. In this blindness, it was as if being the 'descendants of the builders of Angkor' always worked in favour of the leaders of this ancient people, however base and calculating their secret machinations were. The Khmer Rouge had pulled off this tour de force: offering the 'glorious people', bound hand and foot, to the Vietnamese enemy, before making the latter a saviour for winning the war. To top it all off, after they had eradicated Buddhism by killing and defrocking the monks – with the intention of stopping ordinations once and for all – it was the new Hanoi masters who, in 1979, took the initiative of reinstating it in to their country.

In the absence of clergy, Phnom Penh's pro-Vietnamese government, made up solely of former resisters cut off from all else, found itself unable to approve or reject such a political goal that went against Communist doctrine; or even to realise that it was not ancient Cambodian rites that would be restored, but a new composite tradition via an ordaining Vietnamese monk, come expressly from Ho Chi Minh City. A group of seven Cambodian monks were ordained in Phnom Penh's Vat Unalom temple, and these new monks were dispatched directly throughout the country to propagate the new ordination, without the requisite ten years of service . . . The rite that came from this kind of push-button act is not in keeping with the rules of the Vinaya,[3] and, in any case, was invalid. We were witnessing a unique situation in the history of Buddhism, and for many it was a sad sign that a new age had begun in this country. . . .

Poor Cambodia, sterilised at every level by its 'glorious revolution for thousands of years'. The last surviving monks, whom the Khmer Rouge had previously forced to abandon their robes, refused the new rite and let themselves die instead.

A profound need seemed to be arising. But lacking political or religious awareness, what else could the sons of a scattered, disorganised people do – a people whose adults, as rare as they were precious, had rather strive to replant, rebuild, rediscover their culture, to live again? It was the moment when this people of miraculous survivors yearned, at different levels, to raise the country from its ashes, and the inhabitants needed only to regain control of their lives to be reborn.

This was true up until 1992 and the arrival of some 20,000 police, soldiers, civil servants and international experts from the United Nations Transitional Authority in Cambodia (UNTAC), who suddenly took over everything, with earnest-ness and zeal, but with no grasp of mindsets or situations – instantly nipping local initiatives in the bud, exporting the full-tilt effects of civilisation to a country deprived of everything, unhesitatingly corrupting the greediest with the lure of money. Buying back hundreds of UN vehicles that were to be left behind at the end of their on-site mission remained pretty much the only project whose negotiations truly brought together all the local recruits.

The United Nations' special representative officially held the reins of the old kingdom for two years in place of the previous administration, causing an almost immediate wave of discouragement, and wiping out for a long time the ability of the Khmer people to find their soul again. There will be no restoring of what was lost then.

Perhaps after such signs, and in the wake of the stigmas that still tore apart the country, many felt, as I did, a desire to flee from participation in a collective life, especially as it had become clear that future leaders would be recruited from the same cauldron of corrupted humanity.

What words are there today for this country of misfortune? The same words are still in use, even though so much has changed in Cambodian life. Everything may have changed beneath the stilted, dilapidated house, but people go on living in it so as not to have to rebuild it.

*

I am no longer possessive. Before Cambodia I had nothing, afterwards I had nothing left. I freed myself from the ties that long-loved things had imposed on me – because of their beauty, their past, and the memories attached to them. On the other hand, I have never rid myself of the presence of places – of the idea that as the years went by, places stored up wells of tears, the memory of certain moments, events that happened there, as well as the memory of the thousands of beings who had walked across these spaces before they died.

Perhaps that's why I don't like Phnom Penh any more. But it is a confirmation: the places where we lived intensely for a long time always keep attracting us, and I can no more escape that city than I can escape myself. In 1988, I could still find traces of its old architecture in front of the post office, around the Phnom hill, at the freshly rebuilt Hotel Royal, in the big colonial buildings with ruined shutters and no roofs, but still beautiful under their mother-of-pearl sky, and the same iridescent rain clouds. The old metropolis seemed like a long-familiar garden, now abandoned, but still with its distinctive foliage and borders.

On 17 April 1975, before the first Khmer Rouge troops from the north arrived, seeming like children let loose without chaperons, I had seen that same avenue, then totally vacant. In the morning light, it seemed even emptier, deprived of air, to my eyes still tired from the night before. Years later, the French Embassy was still in the state in which the Khmer Rouge had left it in their flight, and I could make out the old setting of its modest buildings in the middle of the park, surrounded by a simple, low wall. The original old gates were still standing next to the sentry box.

Across the way, the banyan of the former Korean Embassy was mummifying, and the *koki* trees had not yet renewed the bark that had been ripped from their knotted trunks by inhabitants for fires to cook their rice. The war memorial was gone; and on the other side, the cemetery had been razed.

At the end of the avenue, the construction site for a wretched government building – encroaching on land freed by the demolition of the cathedral – reminded me that there had been the beginning of the large alley that ran from the train station to the river. It was then planted with flowers and bordered by tall trees of unknown species under which on Sundays the few Cambodian Catholics used to walk as they went to Mass and gave alms to the lepers. I remember that, and the sound of the bells. As for the Buddhist temples of the city that had been invaded by refugees in 1975, they were all still empty.

On the pavements which the Khmer Rouge had planted with coconut palms and along the cobbled streets, there wandered genderless beings with gaping eyes. I began to examine this sorry gathering. Was there any age difference between them? They all looked alike. They all had the appearance and anatomy of individuals raised without love. All beauty, all radiance had left the faces of this population that I had known so cheerful, and in whom passion and desire now seemed dead.

Throughout my old neighbourhood beyond the Calmette Hospital, every stroll held a surprise – occasionally a happy one, like the time when my eyes fell on the iron manhole cover near our house that still resounded with Hélène's dance steps after all these years. And I was aghast to see that the metal had kept the memory to give it back to me, the way childhood memories return to old people.

Other details returned to me, such small things that we barely notice them but which remain hidden behind who knows what back door of memory. I could not forget either all this past time that was regaining life – nor all those ghosts it was so easy to meet during the day, when I would decide to visit the crowded, poorly reconstructed streets, bordered with half-rebuilt houses, an agglomeration of bricks and rubble of all shapes, among the refuse scattered by the rats, and miserable people who scurried by with bent backs. I walked through the labyrinth of narrow alleyways, alongside old houses, without pausing to see who lived there; but I felt their silent presence at the rear of rooms.

It was very hot out, and I sometimes took refuge in my

bedroom in the afternoons; then, at that time when night suddenly invades the city in these climates, when the day is suddenly washed away, I would go to sound out my memories along the Mekong River, in the company of a little group of dogs that followed my example. It seemed to me that important decisions occurred as I was merely drifting along with my thoughts. Perhaps we can weigh up life more clearly in idleness, the melody of things rising up within silences.

The old Japanese bridge and its reflection now formed a single mass hollowed by its arches, while the water of the Four-Armed River moved with the same equal, powerful certainty as ever. Although it was hard to make out the other shore, the space left empty by the demolition of the big seminary was glaringly obvious over the jutting of Chroy Changvar. Despite the curfew, I could walk for a long time without straying far from the sector of the three hotels allocated to foreigners, sometimes walking until the sky turned a diffuse green before the first signs of day.

A few gangs of kids – many of whom were crippled – had escaped from the 'orphanages' and ran rampant in the streets. They never slept, and they bickered amongst themselves like crows; they all seemed to have taken on the colour of crows, too. Each of them had been able to preserve access to the resources of instinct and to the primitive forces of life.

Their stake was the space in front of the three hotels, along with the dividing up of the little one-dollar bills this providential manna generated. The youngest of them could gallop while holding out their hands; the oldest would beg, taking on the voices of ruffians.

A legless boy seemed to rule over the latter. His face was pale and furrowed, and his mouth looked ten years older than he was; only his eyes seemed fragile, squinting at the corners and showing yellowish whites. There was in his gaze such a capacity for attention, such a sense of the nature of others, that it was easy to guess that his childhood had been spent battling against fate.

I came to notice his youth only later on. He was young, young as new Cambodia, where life starts without delay and begins to decline right away. Just the sight of him crushed my heart. He moved from one end of his territory to the other at a surprising speed, by walking on his arms as if they were crutches, his hands in old sandals; and to fight, he forcefully threw his pelvis forward.

I was curious to see him closer up, to talk with him about the past, and I had reckoned, with tears in my eyes, that he might be fourteen or so: his mother had died in labour during the exodus in 1975, an exploding mine had torn him apart thereafter. The idea of the savagery that had become his survival weapon filled me with tenderness.

Several times I let him eat something with me on the terrace of the Sokhalay hotel, which had just reopened. 'How old were you when you lost your legs?' He seemed not to hear my questions, though I could see from his expression that he understood them. He looked so young physically that I was constructing several scenarios when one of the waiters, who had his eye on us and was unable to stand it any more, exposed the subterfuge the boy used with passers by to arouse their pity: he was, in fact, born like that. His bluff unmasked, the kid immediately knew how to behave: he got out of his chair and left without finishing the unfairly received plate, ashamed of not having stepped on a mine like so many others.

The waiter conscientiously turned on his heel, and that was all I needed to understand: at that moment, I confess, I felt the boy had tricked me, as if my credulity had been toyed with. (While it was I who had made everything up myself.) The little charlatan had learned a long time ago that we hold reality in very low esteem, compared to what our daydreams can make us feel.

*

As soon as I started juggling with chronology, as soon as I was ready to walk in the footsteps of this present from which my past escaped, I was allowed to be in another history, another time, without leaving Phnom Penh.

It was in this disturbing negotiation with my own time frame, ever watchful of the familiar journey beneath whatever unknown regions the landscape still harboured, that I walked, one fine morning, into the 'Genocide Museum'. Beyond the barbed-wire enclosure, inside the building, into the classrooms of the former high school, the happy shouts of children who had played in the courtyard were forever smothered by the cries of the miserable people who had been beaten here; the air was still brimming with the superimposed scales of pain that had been played between these walls.

At the time, the administration organised the mandatory visit and provided you with a guide. Would I have gone otherwise? The word 'genocide' as applied to the all-out massacres of Democratic Kampuchea seemed improper to me in the limited sense I gave it; and the shocking word 'museum' made me fear one of those places of political propaganda which the new regime seemed so keen on.

Like everyone else, I did not know that the Khmer Rouge had renamed 'S-21' the former Tuol Sleng school turned prison. In 1979 the refugees did not talk about prisons. So many 'lost' peopled everyone's thoughts that the question of the modus operandi of the death factory – camps, centres, blocks, rooms, ditches, mass graves – remained in the background, even though it had affected everyone. As far as I can remember, people thought that Tuol Sleng had been given prominence by the pro-Vietnamese regime.

Even at the entrance, however, I suddenly stopped short. This hearth of corruption blatantly cried out murder – and murder on a large scale. Simply suspecting the staggeringly high numbers, or having known some individual cases, visitors fell, even collapsed, into acute despondency – such was the aura of suffering surrounding the place. It filled me with such a dread that, for the first time apart from in a Nazi camp, I felt that ontological fear that leaves your blood frozen. As I went in, I withdrew from the world; before the visit was over, I'd experienced torture, learned the extent of its pain, and come to understand that this suffering knows no boundaries. Yet the shocking disharmony that fell upon me was inseparably mixed, and so chaotic, that I could not tell whether the echoing screams came from the men made to suffer or from those inflicting the agony. . . .

The rooms on the ground floor, where the interrogations took place on the yellow-and-white tiled floor itself, were furnished with a tin can (for urine), an ammunition box (for the faecal stream after the first blow), a chair for the interrogator, and a metal bed on which the victim was forced to lie. Living bodies had been split open there . . . All was dilapidated, motionless, long unused, but still vibrating with the cacophony of death rattles, foul breath, confessions withheld and suddenly given, the muffled groaning of the most hardened prisoners, stifled replies.

In the large rooms on the second floor, ghosts escaped from the ragged figures whose photos were on the walls, and the scenario of torture arose so precisely, so unbearably, that I didn't know where to turn. To put up with such sights, I had to hold my breath for so long that I could not prevent the tears from welling up in my eyes. In the absence of all else, the elbow-high scratches on the walls and the wear and tear of the cubicles bore witness to the presence of those who had groped, touched, kneaded their misery there, biting their lips so as to sob less loudly. I read into each corner of these rooms, where dust and blood had accumulated, forming scabs, as an entomologist interprets the remains of insects fragmented by time, the sad hieroglyph of the existence of the people who had run aground here: 'What's the use of doing things and living in this world?'

It was at that very instant that I identified Duch, with an unthinking and absolute certainty, in the photo of the prison director slipped behind the glass of a wardrobe in the reception hall. Keen eyes, teeth that burst from the mouth along the gums' arches, and the pendant lower lip – everything was the same, down to the big ears which I had forgotten and, above all, that subtle bitterness that never left him. At the same time as recognising his unchanged face, I discovered the horrifying extent of his actions from 1975 to 1979, as well as his responsibility in the organisation of torture and executions.

The archives abandoned there showed that the large prison

he was in charge of was designed to occupy a special place in the Party system. The information that was gathered every day here under his watch enabled his leaders to direct their suspicions, and to fight against the 'enemy within'. As before in the Cardamom forest, his work was to find out the plans of the traitors sent to him; and all these detainees had set their eyes on the face of the man who was torturing them – hoping in vain to read in it the answer that they did not know, so as to put an end to their cries. His mission was to channel, unfailingly, the destructive energies conveyed to him by his superiors, before diffracting them throughout the prison population. Such must have been his sense of his commitment to Tuol Sleng, and henceforth the general meaning of his life.

For this purpose, he had set his heart on establishing the rules of a model prison. The aides who carried out his orders, the youngest of whom I had known – I remembered their faces and their teenage zeal in the slightest tasks – had had to learn how to behave as security professionals. In this merciless scenario, he taught them how to use torture with impassivity and in cold blood, without any fits of cruelty, always according to precise rules and with the sole aim of leading the victims to confess. The recommendations he gave them were aimed at ridding them of the idea that beating prisoners was cruel. Pity was not appropriate. Individual cases were irrelevant: the prisoners had to be beaten for reasons of national importance.

As to the victims escorted to death, first before my eyes (I had watched them leave the camp), and later in Phnom Penh, they no longer meant anything to Duch who had quickly become this expert, this 'specialist', this damned soul of the

Angkar for whom the prisoner could no longer mean anything other than an operative field. But in such a scenario, how should one understand the 'exception' that I embodied? How could I accept this 'gift' without feeling guilty, without being an insult to the others' execution? In the suffocating atmosphere that seeped from the former high school's rooms, this question of the pardon I'd been granted by the Khmer Rouge became intense to the point of dizziness.

I now know that Duch had in fact been weakened by my liberation. Shortly thereafter, the arrest of another equally innocent Frenchman, Jacques Loiseleur,[4] proved an opportunity for the apprentice torturer to redeem himself in the eyes of the Angkar. The conditions of his redemption were written within him, in that place inside ourselves that is so hard to penetrate, where the invariables of our true nature take root as early as in childhood.

And the humid, viscous walls of Tuol Sleng showed me the abomination, the ravaging, the torments that 'Comrade Duch' must have force fed himself in order to go on working there. I felt myself shivering as I thought of the brilliant young revolutionary I had known, compared with this possessed being, who remained my fellow man.

Again I saw my ghosts released into the hallways of death and my guts knotted with the fear of escaping them neither seen nor known, like Everyman, secretly reassured by the faith of a new era that must come, confident in the dignity of human beings, the primacy of the spirit, the triumph of moral values. My sole viaticum was a heart full to the brim with all that we long for: to live in a world full of pure, good people who reject war out of love for peace, and death out of love of life; to see the horrors of life smoothed away, as difficulties drift and are resolved in our dreams. . . .

From then on, in what key could I shout the name of the monster of Tuol Sleng without the fear of making the inaudible heard? How could I 'kill the lie without wounding the men'?[5]

IV.

1999 – The Inmate

After the years of turmoil that followed my liberation, and the horrors perpetrated by the rebel group exerting its power, I had persuaded myself that the man who would forever remain labelled 'the torturer of Tuol Sleng' had also disappeared, caught in turn in the meshes of the revolution.

I had to take refuge in Thailand. In the north, in Vieng Papao, I found a Yuan text from the same tradition that I'd started studying in Cambodia. This discovery helped me forget the Khmer Rouge for a while, without alleviating a pain that was now engraved within me, impossible to heal. I settled in Chiang Mai to build the first local centre for the French School of Asian Studies which had become my alma mater, on a beautiful ground that I planted with trees, along the Ping River. From there, I travelled throughout South East Asia – Burma, southern China, and especially Laos – whose traditions all share the same Buddhist background. In that part of the earth, the ancient world was going through a shake-up.

Hélène was with my sister in the French Ardennes; Charles and Laura – two children of whom I'd soon be the father –

would never jump like Hélène had on the backs of giant lizards . . . At the end of the eighties I was offered the opportunity to share my research at Paris's Ecole pratique des hautes études, and thus started a regular 'commute' between Asia and France.

Ten years later, in 1999, I was teaching my classes in Paris, as I did every year in May, when I received a call from Cambodia from a journalist for the *Far Eastern Economic Review*.

'Hello! I have a man opposite me who says he's your friend and that he'd like to see you again. He has some revelations to make, but he'll only talk to you'. [1]

The 'friend' was 'Comrade Duch', whom I had thought was dead. He had fled after the regime's fall in 1979, hiding his identity under different names, like a man who must deny his own shadow. One thing leading to another, he had found a paid job with an American Christian organisation. His new bosses thought highly of the care and efficiency that he had displayed in organising camps for survivors and orphans, near the Thai border.

The former torturer rose up from under the shroud of my fears, out in the open, and now publicly attired in the rags of 'the monster'. But for me the return of this ghost meant much more: Duch was alive, even if one might wonder what kind of a living this was, to be hidden all that time in a grave without a burial permit, and eternally sentenced to remain on the edge of an even more frightening grave – the one dug for him by the victims of Choeug Ek. [2] Yet, as soon as I knew he was alive, all my memories came flooding back.

I had hardly hung up the phone when a whole part of my

past resurfaced in the wake of the call, with the power of an irresistible upsurge. It gave me the impetus to summon the courage necessary to take things up again where I had left them off: as I still could see them, if not as I had experienced them. I pictured to myself Duch somewhere out there, in the Cambodian thickets, incognito and disguised; and I tried to imagine what the daily existence of a post-facto torturer might be like, now that he was drowned in ordinary life, in the midst of others, talking and living again, just like everyone else.

I had already written a few pages in Laos. They opened with the death of my father and with my travails at the French Embassy, and I'd given them a title: *The Gate*. As I remembered it, coming near to death had given me some access to my own father's death, intermingling with it. Without knowing why, I needed to find a hinge between the before and after, between the interior and exterior, elaborating from this idea an image of the embassy's gate through which foreign passport holders had escaped the Phnom Penh exodus in 1975.

But the project had been stillborn. I would have needed to dig deeper, to give it a foothold in the story of my imprisonment, and that already seemed remote, too deeply buried. I had held on to so few memories of Duch that I had lost even the smallest details that bring things to life again. It was as if I couldn't remember anything any more and I needed to recreate everything; I could not count on the stock of images that I had preserved for a while without taking care to fix any in my memory. I couldn't imagine that the fugitive impressions, sensations and emotions that had so briefly affected me in the midst of my moral weakness had in fact left traces that I still bore within me.

The scars left by the ordeal remained scattered, hidden inside me, ready to open again from beneath the rubble among the most forgotten of my secret stratum. Duch's disappearance had slowly melted with the sense of his death; his sudden resurrection, like a breeze carrying the reek of the M-13 camp, reawakened the memory of my meeting, with the man in whose hands fate had brutally summoned me to place my life.

From that moment on, my conscience could find no rest until I recognised, confessed, declared my own truth about what had actually taken place and I had lived through.

*

To write about oneself is to launch into a baroque collage made up of tensions, contrasts, abrupt shifts. It includes a mix of opposing, discordant elements, from which one unearths the fundamental, original relationships, old resentments and minor personal reappraisals. Even if our deeds gradually disappear over time, they remain in a way woven into the web of days. It is possible to see them again, as objects, to describe them, rework them, listen to them again – as with sounds in 'concrete music' – so as to make them more visible, identify their expressive force, spin their thread and rediscover their natural, authentic resonances. I had to take as role models those painters who hate having the model or the subject in front of them, certain of bringing a more profound truth to their pictures by painting from recollection. Present reality is never entirely real until it is consigned to memory.

Taking up the pen also required from me a keener eye than when simply telling a story. The deeper I dug into my soul, the more I dared to express intimate thoughts, and the greater the risk of not finding myself in the words. I had to resign myself first to writing only the 'speakable' truth, before – if I could find the courage – moving on to the unspeakable.

Despite my willingness to go in search of facts, I now found myself very far from the setting of the M-13 experience. Just a few of my thoughts still rambled there, like weird will-o'-the-wisps skimming a swamp of repressions and fixations. The disturbing interaction between Duch and myself only awoke painful feelings within me, like a tearing asunder – a sense of a 'reciprocity' in which each of us had played a role, and that had become hard to understand.

Going back over those impressions meant trusting the endurance of sensations from long ago – past sounds, smells, tastes – the ones that carve themselves in a man as hours go by but that he doesn't bother to take down, just letting what he sees brush against him, overlooking how he feels. It is not possible to forget these fleeting visions, these amoral or high-flying meditations, these sensations-turned-thoughts, once they have interacted with us; they become the true foundation of our ways of being and thinking. They made me write: their swelling opening invisible doors on to myself.

Who was I thirty years earlier when I was set free and left M-13? I was alive, and hence already someone else. Quickly I sensed I had to go back to my sources – but where? Definitely not *elsewhere*, by seeking new horizons. I started instead from what remained of myself: from the young man in Bar-le-Duc, from the SS officer in Nancy who had scared my mother so much she had slapped me, from the women whose heads were shaved at the Libération, from a sparrow that I'd shot down with an airgun from the window ledge of my childhood room – from all these different individuals, these wandering spirits that I was made of, floating like mist about worlds already erased by time, each sketching a shade of my journey. I was this unfinished heap of parts brought back to life in a world that was still familiar and that I was rediscovering as I returned to it, just like a new land that had remained unknown to me.

To write in these conditions was both to suggest that nothing had visibly changed – I had just grown a little thicker and maybe changed a little inside – and also to accept that even though Duch left long ago, he remained there within me, like an egg deposited by an insect. To risk excavating the detestable image of himself that he'd left me with, and to show the world the hereditary features of the human archetype that I did not wish to resemble . . . There was no appeal whatsoever in this perspective.

But isn't every being born to bear witness, and thus express his particular truth? To do so, however, I would have to dive into the innermost regions of myself and find Duch once again, in his natural milieu, the way you reconstruct the prehistoric habitat of a dinosaur based only on the shape of the teeth and the wear of the claws imprinted in layers of schist. I had never seen such a creature from so close up. This contraction in time allowed me to map out a complete outline of his physiology, which I could see unfurling beneath my eyes like an anatomy chart, and to make out all the details rich in meaning, many of which went back to the Creation. I had seen in his lost profile the shadow of a jaw topped by a range of teeth – a feature of monsters, from the oldest to the most recent ones – but this vision had then swiftly eluded any attempt at memorisation.

Without anticipating a goal, I began to write and dig with a mixture of curiosity and anxiety. In the excavated spheres, as in old workshops overflowing with dusty objects, what I had absorbed in the past had the mysterious power to reappear, its meaning intact. I rediscovered the impressions that my senses had photographed of the spectacle of people and things. The multitude of impressions flowed back, the wave of formative energies and elementary images that seemed to fit almost exactly the chronology of events as I remembered them, down to the most unlikely loop. And as I scribbled down phrases, I could see, almost instantly, photos that presented themselves fully developed, as if through years or even decades of a slow, strange process.

I found this work surprisingly enjoyable, even though at the same time I felt dread as I was depicting the expression in Duch's eyes – serious, sorrowful, angry, controlled – when he happened to raise his arm against one of his victims, as children do, except that no one was there to step in and prevent him from striking.

Questions kept running through my mind: how would I have suffered the wounds caused by pincers and cudgels? What is it that chokes the heart and seizes the brain when you're made to swallow a spoonful of chilled faecal matter? More than anything, I tried to guess what his face would look like if he himself had had to torture me; and my own face if, like him, I'd found myself forced to beat those unfortunate people, lying down or weeping at my feet in the prison's half-light.

Actually, since writing involves pinning things down in a way more subtle than is usually necessary, as the sentences followed one another, it grew easier for me to get under the skin of any tyrant, just by following the proper paths; there is no better exercise for laying out plainly the true secrets of our nature. The distance between Duch and me dwindled further; by becoming my own, his evil deeds did not become more acceptable, but they made a lesser impression on me. I was able to grasp by how many imperceptible ties I found myself able to feel a closeness that seemed a priori absurd, and how such ties could not be separated from human traits that nature had endowed me with, as it had him.

An idea came to my mind: the young torturer had made me the keeper of a secret, one that was impossible to expose to broad daylight, like those anaerobic objects that must stay in peat and would not survive in the open air. He had kept me, of all people, alive with the aim of having me as his specific legatee – having decided to finally reveal to someone how all that is incomprehensible and shameful manages to become embedded in a person. I wondered whether, in a decisive moment of his previous life, he hadn't agreed to his fate by casually choosing between many costumes – as if for a fancy-dress party – and as hastily as so many young Nazis had done before him . . . Do we take part in the staging of our own career like an actor in a play whose meaning is beyond him?

I had watched the torturer manoeuvre in order to let me peer, like a voyeur, into his inner morphology. Thus we expose the intimate, the truly unwholesome, to a watcher, and we do not feel overcome by shame; voyeurism in that case only aims at letting him see within us something that he can no longer look at within himself. In the end, the watcher and the watched share the same inner reality.

The fervent revolutionary had opened my eyes to that which I was thousands of miles from suspecting, eradicating any sort of optimism from me. By exposing his distress to me – by taking the chance of lifting the veil from the darkest parts of his being – Duch had knowingly wanted to show me the outline of my own, as one warns a traveller of the perils that lie ahead. He was setting off an alarm whose import and scope was exactly the sort of danger sign he had found lacking on his own journey, but that he did not doubt I would need myself.

Duch had paid the price for what he'd learned from the traps that he himself had not been able to turn away from in time: 'affirmations', 'evidence', 'convictions', 'truths' . . . all this language of 'proof' that rouses men, and makes them cruel. His case allowed me the opportunity to learn much more about myself than I should ever have known in the ordinary world. It was a territory populated with sacrilegious questions.

Some of these revelations came to me as if from the shock of strong spiritual experience, such as those that had astounded Siddhartha (the future Buddha) upon leaving his father's palace. I suddenly found myself in the position of a man who grasps the horror at the heart of all that he has been seeing throughout his days. Despite all the care taken to avoid anything that might show him the true state of things, the Bodhisattva had three encounters: with an elderly person, a sick person and a dead person. For him, all three had provided the dramatic impetus for renewal, a definitive break, and he'd seized the opportunity to meditate on the inevitable grip that suffering holds over each of us and, eventually, to turn his back on the world in disgust.

All things being equal, that was what happened to me when I considered Duch's face: in him I recognised these three apparitions. My meditation was centred especially on the specific nature of human beings, but with an important difference: from a fourth meeting with a religious man, Siddhartha realises that there is a remedy for suffering, but in my case, the suffering I saw in the torturer's eyes left me hopeless.

At M-13, the reality of a world where good and evil were intertwined was perceptible only to him and his entourage. The prisoners noticed nothing during the time they spent there: to them, Duch was no more than a torturer. As for me, during my detention alone I was in no condition to support him in sharing such a heavy burden. Submitting to the general movement and fast changes that drove the camp while I waited my turn, it was impossible to gain enough perspective, or to open myself to hearing that which would resonate later. In his own way, Duch conveyed to me that it was possible to see, understand and even accept necessity, all the while feeling infinite pain. But it took twenty-eight years from the moment when his sepulchral scream first reached my ears for me to begin listening to the message, as if I'd discovered a bottle long ago thrown into the sea. And he would have to bring it to me himself, his spectre coming out of the grave to haunt me.

In *The Gate* I retrace to M-13 my awareness of the so-called shared heredity of the two of us – born of an identical egg, with the same inheritance, the same chromosomes. That view was a parallax mistake stemming from the mysterious reappearance of Duch's ghost. In fact, that feeling was the damaged fruit of an underground labour, like a shadow that fades away as it grows longer; and this work only took shape within me when the book was published and the interviews piled up, as ideas started bubbling in my head.

For example, a question from army cadet Désert[3] suddenly made me think, without elaborating much further, that if there is a true hero down here on this earth, it isn't the person whose courage bursts out while fighting against others, but the one who is capable of showing the courage to battle with themselves – to remain courageous when facing this distorted mirror image of themselves whose threat leaves us with weakened defences.

Sometimes I wondered whether the fact that Duch trusted in me to the point of confessing his crimes was not his way of opening up his heart to someone, in the way that some let down their guard in the middle of a battle, because no friends are left. This man, placed above morality by the laws of war, had imprudently revealed himself to me – so inescapably slippery was the slope on which his idealism already seemed to be sliding.

I now wonder if the lesson drawn from Sarah and my mother's silence did not return to me at the exact moment when I found myself before Duch, flabbergasted and speechless.

*

Duch had remembered me nearly thirty years later, at the time of his arrest, calling me 'My friend Bizot'. I do not think there was ever 'friendship' between us. At the time he could scarcely allow himself that; and I was too dependent on him. Let's not forget that this gentleman's job was to eliminate me, after all! On the other hand, while my liberation had seemed to me as entirely just and nothing else – won despite the vocal hostility of Ta Mok – it turned out to be a dangerous victory for Duch. There was nothing frankly positive for us to celebrate in all this – no joys, no hopes – nothing aside from the fear that had welded us for a few seconds when the situation had suddenly swung into the final straight.

The risk of a last-minute trap had convinced him he should

get a car so as to discourage Ta Mok from having me disappear in the middle of the night.[4] It was in these circumstances, brought closer by a common danger, that we took our leave. And I retain a very clear memory of his fraternal expression at that final instant. Our respective fates were opening up before us as we parted ways by the side of a weakly moonlit path, two inessential parts of a monster machine, from which he could not foresee extricating himself . . .

Of course, I was grateful to him, but not to the point of feeling profound gratitude, perhaps because I was unable to imagine the alternative outcome – that of my execution and demise. Braving death does not make it routine; it distances us from it. From this angle, and despite the extortionate price he had already paid to get closer to hell, I thought of the wretched man as much more destitute than I was. And yet I didn't forget that I too had once been in control of myself and made myself the master of my acts; my behaviour had not been so very different from his in sacrificing the same god, in order to complete the same wish, and giving in to the same shame, against my conscience. I had struck Sarah with a savagery that mingled in my memory with his inquisitor's exertions against his unfortunate victims. On the grounds of reason and the order of things, we'd both tapped into the same primitive ferocity – with the ensuing burden of guilt, yet full of that merciless spirit of decision that drives us to do evil in full awareness. Similarly, we had both hidden from others, apart from a small circle of initiates – my mother and sister for me, and for him, his aides and commanders. I, from fear that others would learn what I had been able to do; he, from fear that some day no one would be willing to believe that 'he too had a heart'.[5]

Countless people around us live in fear that a hidden witness will come forth to remind them of what they once did. This shared sense of pain and shame explains why the ex-torturer might claim he was my friend, while I called him only my brother.

Today, returning to those years of meditation seems all the more important since my thoughts set loose by Duch sometimes awoke fear among the optimists, that 'great fear of the self-righteous'[6] before which everyone freezes: in Man we trust, only insofar as he shows the acceptable face of who we swear we are.

When I lived in Srah Srang, the Khmers – who knew better than anyone how to look straight at human nature – had already triggered my suspicions. During their coming of age, before being considered men, the boys were called 'those who are not yet afraid' (*min'ten ches khlac*). As such, they had to practise meditation to defeat the personal enemy said to lie within, as a demon, with the aim of attaining maturity and wisdom eventually. Such rituals, destined to bring the child into the desperate world of men, had immediately warned me of dark prospects for humankind. But in truth, it wasn't until after my initiation at the hands of my torturer that I understood the aim of this ancient rite: to initiate the village youth into fear of themselves.

*

I made contact again with Duch in 1999, after he had been arrested. I sent my questions to him through his lawyer, Kar Savuth, and his replies would come back to me by mail, written with care on the back of the same sheet.

He had a one-room lodging on the ground floor in the courtyard of the military building where they held him. The door and shutters remained closed at night; his regimen was stern, though carried out good-naturedly by his guards, and he had to survive in great destitution. A few feet away from him was his former leader, Ta Mok, who was being held in the same prison. Unlike Duch, Ta Mok had amassed vast sums of money. The old man, while sick, enjoyed some comfort there and ordered his meals from restaurants. In view of the rivalry between the two men, which had almost cost me my life but of which I was nevertheless the source, and after having dilly-dallied for weeks, burdening myself with almost unbearable syllogisms – the former torturer had helped me, should I help the former torturer? I finally made up my mind to have a 100 dollar bill sent to Duch; solving a morally insoluble problem in this way, without offending public sentiments, caused no one any harm.

On 24 January 2000, having just returned from a quick excursion in the Cardamom foothills where I had been able to find the debris of the former camp by the stream, I set out early in the morning for Tuol Sleng. I had already returned there on several occasions in the meantime, like an onlooker joining the researchers who were sorting through the archives. As the visits went by, I had grown to know the museum's staff members, who were joined on certain days by one or the other of the seven prisoners who had managed to escape the jail. Some came to make a little money by acting as tour guides. They had known Duch from afar, but that day everyone was talking about the incident that had happened the day before, as if a tragedy had narrowly been averted.

'You only just missed his son!' they said to me, laughing.

Duch's son had in fact come to the ticket booth, looking for his father.

At the time of the Vietnamese victory, on 6 January 1979, Duch, his wife and their two children, the younger barely three weeks old, had taken flight barefoot. Two other boys were born thereafter, the youngest in 1986. This last child was seventeen years old by then and living in his grandparents' house in Skuon (Kompong Thom). He had learned that his father was interned, and had also heard that he had run the central prison of Tuol Sleng; connecting these two pieces of information together had led the son to take the bus to Phnom Penh.

The high-school student was from the country and not very self-assured, and his complexion was white and delicate like his father's. A moto-taxi had dropped him off at the former prison's barbed-wire gate, just as the first cars were entering the central courtyard and foreign visitors and their guides were calling to each other and crowding together in the entrance area. The young man had mingled with the crowd.

The ticket-collector had made him repeat himself several times before realising that he was the torturer's son. Immediately, she had motioned for him to be quiet and had led him to the rear pavilion where the museum employees gathered.

'Shh!' she said, taking his hands and having him sit down. 'You shouldn't say who you are, or speak your father's name. Don't you realise? It's dangerous . . . They could take it out on you. A lot of people died, you understand?' she pleaded with him, full of pity, surrounded by employees elaborating on her statements and making sure that no one else approached. 'Your father is not here. He is being held in the military prison, thirty minutes away.'

Duch's youngest son stayed for a bit, staring at a glass of tea, and then someone walked him away to be sure that he wasn't being followed, even travelling part of the way with him, in the direction he'd take to find his father.

*

As soon as *The Gate* was published, I formed a plan to see Duch again, but he wasn't permitted any visits. At any rate, he did not want any visitors apart from his children, his confessor and, he added, me. The reversal of our roles was a curious thing to behold, and I could see that in his thoughts, my part had little by little outgrown the one he had taken in my own story: in the private court of his conscience, wasn't I the sole moral alibi that he could call on?

Still, I didn't expect much from his 'disclosures', even if it might have been interesting to know the background of the stage upon which my life had been decided with a roll of the dice, or to have heard from Duch's mouth in what exact circumstances he had given the order to have my companions Lay and Son killed. My real interest followed an entirely different path. While I was not indifferent to his wish to speak with me, my aim was not to renew ties with an old acquaintance – between our pasts and presents – but to continue with him an interior dialogue that I had never been able to interrupt. I wanted to understand what had happened in his head, and also in his heart; to go back over the events as he saw them. Talking freely with him seemed the only way to open new perspectives on myself.

I had asked that a copy of *The Gate* be given to him quickly. His lawyer assured us that it was something that could not be refused and I was so curious about what he might think as he read me, to hear his words instead of my own, to hold my account up against his own recollection (even if it might mean writing an addendum for future editions), that I had even ascertained this right from the high authorities.

Of course, I didn't think that he would willingly return to events the mere mention of which seemed already to revive sacred taboos. Thinking of his recent religious conversion, if one translated his staggering experience of the death and suffering of others into Christian terms, it wasn't difficult to appraise the immense weight of his distress. No, if Duch was going to morally allow himself to look back at his past, he would need a higher revelation – a more powerful trauma than a mere conversion from one faith to another – and I thought that the confrontation between us, our two lives, might eventually serve as the release.

In any case, I just wanted to see him again for no specific reason, or no reason that I could explain to myself. There was nothing personal to it. Perhaps I wanted to meet him as Gitta Sereny had the commander of Treblinka,[7] or Hannah Arendt during the Eichmann trial,[8] to listen to him give his own summing up of his fall, along the lines of Rudolf Hoess's confessions[9] – whose personal reflections and intimate observations could be compared, with some subtle differences, to the notes Duch sent to me.

Conversely, a curious fact, and one hard to express, is that the particular interest I had in meeting him seemed disembodied, detached from him, now that Duch was there – aware and alive, bearing his cross. I felt that his fate was of little interest to me, or in any case becoming of less and less interest.

I probably expected something else from this man, and in the end much more than he could give: a second liberation. Without either seeking or finding excuses for him – that wasn't really the issue – I needed to look at him up close. I was anxious to emerge once and for all from the state of perplexity and doubt which had been disturbing me since his reappearance. Namely, I needed to know what it meant to still be a 'human', living in such conditions.

Obsessive, unbearable thoughts came to me, as if there were things that we could only think about by pushing to the limit, as if some fundamental philosophical secret surrounded Duch, which had taken time to be dug, to deepen, but about which he remained silent because no one could hear it any more. My mission on this level was to be able to approach him without disguise, as I had already done, but this time to push the confrontation to its conclusion, beyond words – to get to his mystery, reach the soul beneath his intelligence. I wanted to be with him in a room without speaking.

*

It was on the occasion of the shooting of a documentary film[10] about the events mentioned in *The Gate*, that, on 21 February 2003, the right to talk for a while with Duch about issues that 'were pertaining to the facts' was granted to me.

I should say that in the meantime I had become afflicted, perhaps from age, with a kind of sensory confusion in which the brain sniffs out ahead of time those I was to meet or touch, just as others may have an abnormally acute sense of smell, reluctantly detecting the miasma exhaled when in the physical proximity of other beings. Touching the hand of Duch was hard to imagine; it would be to risk contamination with his infamy, with the spurts of blood of the tortured, with that fine substance that still covers the walls of Tuol Sleng and that sticks for ever to the skin of torturers. It would be to make myself guilty by association and to take part in the scenes of torture, as if to relieve him proportionately. Simply to smile in his presence already seemed a dubious mark of complicity to me. I counted on that strange phobia – risen from the depths of time – to protect me from the dangers of such a detestable contagion.

The interview took place in a sun-filled room that served as a visitors' room, in the presence of a clerk and two military judges. They had me sit down while waiting for the prisoner. The exact order was that I should have no physical contact with him. But when Duch came in with his two guards, seeking me out, I was the one who got up with my hand outstretched towards the frail, surprisingly aged frame – shaken by this strange figure surging from my memories. The former Khmer Rouge soldier returned my gesture in an absent-minded way, but I read in the disciplined expression of his eyes that he had been expecting me to greet him from a distance. A certain confusion gripped me at the rugged touch of this man who had saved my life and whom I had long ago buried in my subconscious. I scrutinised his face for a long time from close up, doubtless with the same avidity as I had earlier when I'd arrived at the camp. But this time I was trying to uncover what was new in it. It was as if my gaze had landed on the recent photograph of a singular being that I recognised, but who wasn't the one I had grown used to seeing in my recollections. This face's transformation was thus doubly striking: I instantly regained lost impressions – but at the same time I was thoroughly surprised by its features.

A blinding ray of light pierced the fine dust that his entrance had raised in the room. I asked about his living conditions, the way prisoners talk with one another: 'How is it here, is it OK?' I felt how odd my question was and I had to repeat it to make myself understood.

'Hmmm . . .,' he said, without listening, shaking his head. 'I wouldn't have recognised you.'

'Bizot!' I insisted, pointing to my chest.

'I know. I often thought again of you at the time . . . I was twenty-nine years old. I was born in 42.'

I was thirty-one.

'I thought that we were the same age.'

'No.'

'Ta Mok would not show me the report that had come from above. We didn't say Pol Pot, we said "Above". Actually, it was the order for your release. And I remember on Christmas Eve, we'd drunk coffee without sugar! Afterwards, on the road, I didn't know any of the four people in the car. At one point, we took a detour and I was very scared.'[11]

Duch's forehead no longer bore the slightest trace, not the least reflection, of the powers I had known him to have. On the other hand, the secrets brought back from a long stay in the house of the dead had placed a heavy weight on his appearance – it was a stupefying vision. With the bitterness expressed by the fine network of wrinkles on a face that had revealed itself to me when so young there now mingled little, brown, impressionistic touches that streaked his temples, bringing out the shadow of the lines of his fate. And his physiognomy now showed things I had not known about him. He looked like one of those figures stamped on a medal, which you can also make out on the reverse. The unease at finding himself in my presence lent him a demoniac expression; as my eyes searched him out beneath the rust-like stains on his skin, reminiscent of ancient blood splatters, his features slowly relaxed and a hint of emotion seemed to spread on his face. Did this man still possess, even after Tuol Sleng, an inner life and heart that no one, except me, cared to look into? At that very moment, I was able to identify in the unusual composition of his face that of the man I had known, and I remembered that this figure of evil had not always shied away from goodness. And I could neither marvel at nor be terrified enough by the idea of all those twenty years of flight he had been able to bluff his way through – his hand on a switch, one moment dark and prickly, the next mild and docile like those predators that choose to live amongst their prey.

We sat at the end of the table. Nodding his head, Duch repeated that he might have passed me by in the street without recognising me. The judges allowed him only to talk about certain precise facts, such as the circumstances of my liberation, which I already knew, or of Lay and Son's deaths. I was curious to learn if he had received the thirteen volumes of Marx's *Capital* and the little stock of quinine pills that I had paid the Udong soldiers to pass on, on behalf of Lay and Son too . . . In fact, we mostly looked at each other: I, thinking about him much more than I was listening to him, and he ensnared by images from the past which came back to him in new forms.

When the time came to leave him, I was overtaken by a sort of disinterest, an indifference, and had the sudden impression of being in front of someone utterly foreign, whose fate left me cold. I no longer felt any of the effects that the first moments of our reunion had produced in me, and I abruptly realised that I had just seen him 'alone': his being, his person, everything about him had become alone – so alone that he seemed to have created a void in the room.

This was never the impression he gave at M-13. Duch always lived under strict control, as if he were fed on a drip, constantly linked to the tight mesh of the great web that had been woven for him and that identified him, as it does spiders. The whole of his action was part of an ideology from above and from the spirit of his peers. But there in his cell, the spirit of this prisoner no longer came from anyone. The M-13 man had left the inmate; the two were no longer linked, unless grouped with his erstwhile comrades.

What if it all came down to this: the space between a no man's land and promiscuity? I mean, the paradox of that passage between a person alone and a person in a group, between what one does individually and what drives us collectively? Honestly, who are we really dealing with once the torturer has been plucked from the rat-hole and is free from the loathsome mechanisms that had plunged him into it? You expect the devil and instead you find a destitute being, with no memory, no papers, no luggage, who only wishes for one thing: to change lives.

If the importance of a sensation can be measured by the anxieties and sorrows that go with it, then it struck me that I had already felt in my youth what I was feeling at this moment. This impression reminded me of one of my themes from a time when I often used to think that the natural thing for our remote ancestors was to live one day at a time, to die at night and be reborn the next day. When it came, death would take them at night like a wave, without their noticing it. Perhaps fully existing was limited for them to daytime activities, and life after death was only that of dreams. No day after, no retribution, no guilt. No plans either, and so none of those long-term collective undertakings that call for calculations, promises and a large number of dead. Modern man only asserted himself later by creating a link between his previous frustrations and the allure of the future. . . .

Being seventy-one years old now, and having long ago entered the time of doubts, I am aware of having constantly wavered between these two indissoluble states: on the one hand, an openness to the moment, to the sensation of the coming second – that timeless sparkle whose artifice I hold dear and which distracts me from tomorrow's worries – and on the other hand, the ever-changing images, the systematic invasion of abstractions that cut me off from a joyfulness which then becomes out of reach. The carefree present, the worries of the future – each like a drug that makes me forget the other.

When the judges directed the guards to take Duch back to his room, he suddenly became animated like a schoolboy when the recess bell rings. He abruptly asked – the way you try to get important information quickly from just a few words – how Hélène's mother had died, a death I vigorously denied since she was in France. A great surprise came over him, as if the survivor had performed what he would not have thought her capable of. Then he wanted to know how I had managed to smuggle her out and, without taking the time to breathe, asked Hélène's new name – assuming that she must be married – as well as the names of her children. . . . And every time I had to go back over my replies, since he wanted so many other details. I'd had to promise him a picture of me and Hélène, to put in his cell.

*

After the discussion, I'd found my head incredibly empty, as if I had retained nothing from those two hours of communication, exchange and impressions. The cameramen were waiting outside for me to emerge and the only feeling I could share with them was my surprise at not having seen Duch smile one single time. . . .

By a stroke of luck, the first few minutes of the meeting had been filmed; contradicting what I said, the rushes showed the prisoner freely displaying his joy at seeing me again. I had simply projected my concerns on to him, presuming that, broken by so many trials, the executor of Tuol Sleng's highest tasks could no longer smile. . . .

This bit of film also demonstrated the instinctive sympathy I had shown for this man who was now facing his crimes with the same rigour he had previously displayed in all things – without pride, but with brave looks, like a repentant child who resorts to honesty to make a better show of his sincerity . . . all the while knowing that the most zealous of his accusers would be the ones who would sentence him while asking themselves the fewest questions.

*

I took the film crew to search for the place where they had once chained me up, at the heart of the special zone in the 'Southwest Region', right in former Khmer Rouge territory. The prison visit had made me lose my bearings; I needed to retrieve the past by walking on the ground of old, the better to return to Duch by the very path where I had left him.

Surrounded by bamboos, the premises had remained as sinister as in the memories that awoke in me. Being there immediately gave me grounds to escape from my denial and repressions, and I took much comfort in recognising those tall columns that had served as my shelter. I had the map that Duch had sent to me, and the name of a town that was easy to locate. A former Khmer Rouge supporter from this sparsely inhabited area came to show us the way. My young son accompanied us on the trail of the man who had saved his father-to-be. Here and there, ruined copses of dark woods cut into the arid expanse of undergrowth but the forest was now so dry that nothing matched the image I still bore of it.

The dilapidated forest had kept none of the sudden rises I had known; and the fact that those old trees had disappeared little by little from the view on this earth was the saddest of all omens. At that season, the slow stream escaped noiselessly from the bamboo, between the rare ferns. As for the beautiful plant species of the undergrowth, whose outlines I had not forgotten after all these years, I noticed that, apart from the striking rattan palmtree, whose prehensile shoots kept sticking to my guards' shirts, what grew in the shadows had not grown much, while other common, less interesting species had grown more quickly. The opal tree under which I had been tied now stood taller, drier, and waxier. It was from here that I had first heard the distant shrill of my friend the oriole. But after a few minutes in the shadow of its high crown, as if my eyes had finally exhausted the secrets of the visible world, a dust made of death and crumbling bones began flowing over the dirty ground. Although nothing had been buried here in a long time, the stench of evil still floated over the place.

*

On the way back, we stopped to meet Duch's family: his mother, his sister, and especially his only daughter, twenty-six years old and born in Tuol Sleng, the eldest of his four children who had made a strong impression on everyone. I couldn't stop myself from saying that it was thanks to her father that my own daughter still had one. 'Once,' I told her, 'when I was his prisoner, your father, who wasn't married yet, said to me: "One day maybe I too will cry, not knowing where my child is." Have you been to see him in prison?' She said she would travel to Phnom Penh. I know that she did not go.

V.

2009 – The Defendant

The question has been haunting me for forty years: did I ever contribute in any way to this fate that makes me one of the only witnesses at the Khmer Rouge trial able to look at Duch with tragic concern? The question gnawed at me and grows stronger every day.

Perhaps it's because my life began in this radical struggle with a loathed enemy – that was said to be absolute – and that I lost my innocent view of the adversary thereafter. Did this happen in Algeria, when I wondered how I myself could turn into 'the enemy'? I no longer picture the enemy as being so different from me; even if that doesn't prevent me from execrating him just as strongly. Duch became the main witness and touchstone of this tearing asunder, this private contradiction, the best prism I could use to get a glimpse of myself.

I saw him again once, with Judge Lemonde, in his new prison's high-security section area: four cells facing each other, on either side of a corridor. That day the interview dealt with commonplace comments, and we discussed *The Gate* and the note he was writing with his impressions on the book.[1] For an instant I was vividly aware of being able to read in his appearance that which is usually hidden from our understanding: the tipping point where things go wrong. And I could fathom how this evil that happens to us comes into us, through us, from us . . . Only this facet of the individual, of our fellow man, is likely to open our eyes to the suffering of the world.

*

On that morning of 8 April 2009 – as I found myself in a car assigned to escort me, under protection of one of the bodyguards of the 'Support Unit for Witnesses and Experts', caught in traffic jams on Route 4 – the same questioning rang on in my head with an intensity that increased hour by hour. I knew that, after I had crossed the threshold of the court, these interrogations would remain – anchored more deeply in me – the only reality, the only thought that matters when facing the field of the dead.

I had received the 'summons to appear' in Chiang Mai a few days earlier, when I was no longer expecting it. The magistrates had made up their minds at the last minute to hear me as witness for the court – that is, with no link to either party. At first, Duch's legal assistants had suggested that I speak as a defence-appointed 'cultural expert'. This was an unhoped-for opportunity to make a connection with him, to speak more freely and frankly with him, to let things come from within, if indeed any relationship of trust could ever be nurtured in the visiting room of a prison. Actually, this man to whom I wanted to get closer, whose dreadful secrets I imagined myself probing – I felt that I only knew him in certain ways, in the things we shared; the rest was a mystery . . . But I turned down the offer:

what I had to say about human nature ran the risk of being construed as a sort of 'guilty plea', an appeal for forgiveness, which the defence lawyers were liable to use as mitigating circumstances. I could not allow my recruitment by the defence to have people believe that I wanted to bypass the horror or belittle the suffering of the victims. I had to find a way to go beyond Duch as a person, and to maintain a distance in order to make myself better heard.

That is why I had no objection to the prosecution summoning me to appear. For me, accusing Duch wasn't so much pointing the finger at *this* man as exposing Man himself. In either case, I would be saying the same things. The co-prosecutors, however, eventually decided not to call me. All of these delays, these stops-and-gos, spaced out over weeks, explained why I hadn't closed my eyes for several days, and why I was stricken with fear before my appearance in court. I spent the night thinking, jotting down words, without being sure of anything, and I wrote up a little checklist, to keep at hand in case a name, date or place went missing from my memory.

We arrived on time – at 8 a.m. – despite the traffic jams and reached one of the entries to the vast fortress. We parked the car between round buildings with pointed roofs, in line with a door leading to a hallway from which a bundle of thick electric cables jutted out, falling loose in places. There was a pagoda made of cement in the courtyard that sheltered some god of the earth, from a lost pantheon, that stood holding a metal hammer and pointing a threatening finger; witnesses would be brought to kneel before it and take an oath, reminiscent of the rites of the old court's two Neak Tas,[2] during the French Protectorate.

I was immediately led through various offices up to a sort of hidden, airless storage room beneath a staircase. I was supposed to stay there at the ready, but I would have run right away had it not been for a law student from the former East Germany next to me, appointed by the court to escort the witnesses. At that instant, I would have given anything not to walk into that torment. I had the horrible sensation of being there to commit a crime against humanity. . . .

Testifying before the court. Reporting how I crossed paths with the defendant. Confronting an audience that was waiting for just one thing to protest and pounce: that I paint a human portrait of the killer, by which I would be suspected of explaining, understanding, and thus excusing – whereas my confusion arises precisely from the impossibility of pitying, and even more of absolving, him. In short, great as the charges were against him, and even greater the horror his action aroused in me, I would not disown the empathy experienced in the forest of Omleang. Deliver the most secret of my thoughts, despite the voices that would speak up in the name of reason. Free myself from all taboos, not run away from questions, plant myself firmly in front of what I am not ashamed of believing, find the words from my nights of insomnia, reveal what I saw one day and what I see again constantly. Reassert, at the risk of being accused of heresy, the truth from which we have been backing away since the beginnings of time: the monster's humanity.

*

I was already familiar with the new law courts, including the courtroom itself, with its benches arranged in an elliptical arc and its light wood furnishings, where the clerk's desk, the prosecutor's bench, the witness box, the Bar, face the highest seats reserved for the judges, with all of them separated from the gallery reserved for the audience by a wall of glass panels. I had been there the year before, during the judicial investigation, then at the very beginning of the trial, before the official announcement of my appearance.

Hélène wanted to take advantage of the occasion to see Duch in the flesh at least once in her life. His figure remained the epicentre of an earthquake that had devastated her childhood, that of her oldest memories and her first fears. After keeping up appearances for a long time, she too had to come to grips with reality: to accept the fact that the man to whom she can never be too grateful for having saved her father was also a killer who made a multitude of others die. He himself had only ever seen her in photographs. One morning, as the audience and the journalists were arriving and looking for seats, we both discreetly walked over to the stand, and, for a few seconds, Hélène stood there, in front of the security window, so that Duch could see her. My 'liberator' thus had a chance to observe my daughter and to respond to her wave. *What would have become of me without him?* she thought, looking at the torturer.

None of this escaped the attention of the people sitting just behind us in the first row, among whom were the French ambassador who looked offended, and one woman in particular, a Frenchwoman. A little later, she came to greet me. Her husband had been killed in Tuol Sleng like all the others, but for her he was the only one. She'd come to testify, in the memory of the father of her children and the man whom she still loved. She told me how hellish her life with her daughters had become. She saw Hélène, she'd read my book; she told me she understood, but she just wanted me to know that her heart was breaking. *What would have become of us without him?* she thought, looking at the torturer . . .

*

A bell rang. The door of the little room opened and the bailiff told me to follow him down a dark passageway and I entered the stage with fear in my belly, as if I were the prisoner: before me were dozens of people in absolute silence . . . In the middle of the brightly lit, airtight, trap-like space – whose stifling atmosphere I'd have to endure – it occurred to me that other layers of a more harmful presence awaited me. The torturer's tragedy was apparent in a very personal, individual, catastrophic way; I was reminded that I too had a place somewhere in this drama, that I had to answer for myself and for others.

In the spectacle on the theme of 'humanity accused' that was playing out, Duch had the part of the fallen being: indicted for having done evil while wanting to do good. We can only purge ourselves of the tragic through tragedy itself; in eternal wars against the same enemy, apart from our great magical ceremonies of expelling evil, theatre is our only recourse. There has to be a lot of dramatisation to take hold of a being and extract him from his time, with the aim of banishing the devil hidden within him. But however I interpreted the scene in court, I could already hear singing and dancing in the room, ready for the exorcism of the beast.

A few feet away from where I went to sit, Duch was standing amid his guards, a stranger to himself, consenting to the forces of justice, ready to collaborate, aware of the evil assigned to him, feeling that it was in him, in his own being – that it had all indeed happened. He was leafing through a file, leaning over to hear something, but his eyes didn't stray from me and were full of expectation. For a brief instant, I saw in them such a visible anguish that I forced myself not to meet them. Yet I had seen there the same semblance of pride he had had on the last night before my release, during dinner, as he'd listened to me answer his leaders' questions.[3]

Now, the exhalation of his victims' breath, resurfacing during the questioning, kept him from breathing. For some time fate had abandoned him to the exhaustion that makes killers fall. His pupils were no longer narrowing in the distant light of that azure of the promised land that had fled from him – as it has always slipped away from man, when the vanishing point of his horizon is set too low beneath the surface of the sky. And although all his comrades died before disenchantment and disgust had set in, Duch watched me walk up to the stand. I was the last witness of that time when the courage that drove him to live was born of hope, before it became despair.

Yet my account also accused him: without me M-13's many crimes would have remained in the shadows. And – since it is true that we see things more clearly when they rise up in front of us – such a great amount of anguish, shame and suffering oozed from his being, combined with a poignant need to see the truth come to light, that I suddenly felt as if the crowd's hatred and screams were swelling my stomach with nausea.

*

Under the raw light aimed at me, the bailiff led me to the spot reserved for the witness. He showed me how the microphones worked, their red light going on, as well as the overhead projector, the flat screen and the headphones linked to the interpreters. I unfolded my list of words to remember; in my briefcase there was, as evidence, the yellowed notebook that Duch had given me to write in, along with a copy of *The Gate*.

I needed to settle and gather my thoughts, yet I was in a state of almost hostile agitation, and I sensed stage fright in my trembling fingers. In the court, the atmosphere was heavy but free of aggressiveness. The presiding judge had the dark complexion of a villager – and blue lips and dull teeth – which inspired confidence in me. The attitude of the other magistrates and lawyers seemed equally affable. Most disturbing at first were the long pauses, the excessive slowness with which each person spoke, the delays with no obvious cause, all of which made me make the mistake of beginning my testimony before the clerk had read me the oath. I noticed the hesitant translation from French to Cambodian, to say nothing of that from Cambodian to French. Moving in my chair, I glanced through the glass, out at a packed public gallery from which rose a muffled hum that seemed to come from far away.

In the silence of these peasants bused in every day by the victims' associations – and aside from a confusion that no further surprise could make any worse – I could sense that personal defence mechanisms were gone. This mute world was simmering in a strange mixture of hostility, anxiety and pent-up grief – not emerging for one moment from the nightmare it was still living through. Many still bore on their faces the stigmata of the death they had barely escaped, and they all shared a rage against the living symbol of those who'd killed Khmers in such vast numbers. The sight offered to them sent them back into the world of butchers which they had all discovered thirty-five years earlier with the eyes of innocent, frightened children.

No one can give a name to the forces that clash with each other once you've entered the courtroom; the public, the defence, the prosecution, the guilty man and the magistrates stare fixedly at each other. The improbable combination of distance and proximity spontaneously freed the powers of hate. The most terrible part was the public description of the tortures inflicted on victims by the defendant: the long throes of suffering rushed at us, and we felt our wounds throbbing from within, as if they were speeding towards us 'from the deepest part of our reflection in the mirror'.[4]

For everyone here the killer was the symbol, in its most malevolent form, of the disaster that had pounced upon the land of the Khmer and all its inhabitants – the earth, house, father, mother, wife, husband, dead child. As I write these lines, I can hear the violence exploding in the hearts of those close to me and of the children of my dead friends, who came to look at the murderer, to memorise his face, to catch a glimpse of his expression, to grasp for ever whatever evil emanation there was in the face of a man who did not even know them. They were all impatient to exact their revenge, to excrete the overflow of their pain, to re-route it, to evacuate it by the only channel available to everyone: that of vengeance – to send the evil back, as the magician turns an evil spell back upon its source.

If there is something inhuman about a courtroom, it is definitely this operation of justice on people's suffering. Laws can't console anyone when the tears spring from within. The magistrates are involved on each side – embracing the victims' claim, considering the defendant's rights, splitting hairs, deliberating on the basis of some accounting average that is the fruit only of mental calculation . . . And the tragedy of the constantly frustrated victims stems from this; from this, the tragedy of the forever misunderstood guilty party. Hence the lawyers' impossible mission: the prosecutors who refuse to see the man before focusing on the murderer; and the defence lawyers who cloak the murderer in order to allow us to better see the man. Hence the inevitable betrayal of the magistrates, in a comedy that might be a farce if the aim weren't to reassure the public and free us from our fears.

The error lies in our determination to consider people from the outside, following a thought-process that urges us to give physical form to metamorphoses drawn from the depths of our imaginations; this propensity to reduce discourse to schematic oppositions, to close in on itself by denying reality; this temptation to stifle voices that contradict and explain to us why 'eating the fruit of the tree of knowledge was a risk of falling, a loss of real life'.[5] I take exception to this self-righteous, rationalised, institutionalised conscience, on which we force our children to base their lives.

It makes me wonder if we will ever see international criminal courts – subjected to such pressure since they are windows that open upon our true face – proceed one day with inquiries into crimes *against humanity* by daring to attack 'mankind', and going beyond trying just 'one man'.

If recognising a killer usually means distinguishing him from other beings, recognising the person responsible for a heap of tens of thousands of piled-up bodies is first realising the species to which he belongs. Specific memories blur when faced with such images; in the case of an individual murder, my perception stays on particular features; it eludes me when it comes to mass killings. I feel I am a part of that unity, I feel it in me; and because of it that I exist.

Still, it seems to me that my entire life has been spent listening to the cry of the killer rise up from the depths of the earth. A nausea seizes me that will not go away, like my anguish in the cold of the railroad tracks at the Bar-le-Duc station. Will we always be too frightened to recognise that instant of truth, to understand that the human being who raises his arm against his fellow does not exist separately? He makes the crime his own in the only way there is: by crying out in order to draw from its source the cruelty he needs – like the sheep butcher in the Nancy slaughterhouse, who mistreated, insulted, terrorised his inoffensive victims, urged on by the necessity to gather all his strength. In Thailand, the torturer goes about things differently; he kneels at the foot of the condemned man with a bouquet of flowers before executing him. (Somewhat as I had done with the pigs in Srah Srang.) Ferocity, compassion – each and every one of us performs the great leap forward in our own way, according to our rank and milieu, sometimes upstream and sometimes downstream from our own fright.

Beneath our feet, next to giant dragons, are rotting caves where the spirit of age-old times moves; grottos filled with bones, the bodies of our ancestors mixed in with their prey, and no space between them.

*

'Were you arrested by the Khmer Rouge and interned in the Kompong Speu Province in 1971?'

'That's correct, Your Honour.'

I'd sworn to myself the night before that I would mention straight away the fate of M-13's prisoners, and recall Lay and Son's names at the outset of my testimony. Now, as soon as they were awakened, the images passed before my eyes, like a comic strip that I had begun to read.

The instant I mentioned my first encounter with the young Khmer Rouge torturer, and while I was in the field of vision of the defendant and he was seeing the same images go by, I experienced a strange twofold time, when the sadness that already overwhelmed his features seemed a premonition to me.

Later on in my account, when I mentioned a teenage soldier who came to sing to us a melody inspired by Chinese revolutionary music, in his beautiful soprano voice, which we had both listened to dreamily, I saw Duch slowly freeze on his bench, nodding his head, as if this memory cheered his heart more than he'd believed was still possible . . . The young singer had sat across from us, shyly. 'The sound came effortlessly out of his half-open mouth, drawn like ink across a page, light and fragile, trembling and delicate. Is there any emotion more poignant than that inspired by words of love and hatred, sung by a child? There was such purity in his silvery voice, weaving between the stars, that every syllable was wreathed in eternal beauty.'[6]

My testimony went on for hours and didn't end until the noon break. I don't know how stress allowed me to hold out: I had to speak in a stifled voice, caught between the emotion of the memories that still disturbed me and the horror of the crimes I still saw, without ever for a second leaving the field of vision of the man it all stemmed from. I felt I was choking under the pressure of the same fate as him.

From that point on I thought I was finished, but it was the turn of the lawyers from both sides to question me. Immediately after lunch, my interrogation began.

*

Strangely, the presiding French judge spent quite a long time examining the documents that the guerrillas had given me for the French Embassy. These documents, which I didn't remember in detail, contradicted a theory (in favour among certain historians as well as former Communist leaders in the Hanoi camp) which claimed that the Cambodian revolutionaries did not have a political programme at that time (the end of 1971). What can I do about that? The photographs and two documents duly submitted to the French Embassy's chargé d'affaires were lost in Phnom Penh; and if my translation of them had been the subject of a diplomatic telegram to Paris, it was in such abridged form that one could only make out their broad outline. The passage concerning the changes in society planned for the future, which seemed to especially interest the judge, is not mentioned. I don't know if these cuts were due to the censorship that the diplomatic post was trying to exercise at the time, in line with the orders from the Foreign Affairs ministry, which was rather favourable to the Khmer Rouge option. To tell the truth, the debate leaves me cold. Still, I could see its import in the context of the trial, and I was reassured to hear Duch confirm in front of the court that I had in fact been given two texts relating to the 'Party's Political Programme' following a meeting headed by Ta Mok.[7]

The lawyer then asked for permission to question the defendant directly in relation to an extract from my book.

During the time it took for the request to reach the presiding judge in Khmer, and for him to consult the other magistrates, I had an opportunity to look the defendant in the eyes and to take the whole measure of a situation where our respective roles were reversed.

'Good . . . Can you hear me? I am going to read you a passage where the witness reports what you told him.'

I was thunderstruck, dumbfounded; I could hear nothing more. As I had guessed, it was the episode when I accused him,[8] when he let go of his secret, his eyes wide open – the way one talks in psychoanalysis – and he had confessed his duty to me and the violence that motivated his actions.

The magistrate slowly read the passage into the microphone . . .[9]

'Do you agree with this transcription? Do the words attributed to you come close to the truth?'

My God! Those may not be the exact words that had come out of his mouth, which he himself surely couldn't remember . . . But I did convey the exact tone – the breath, the voice, the silence surrounding us – all that can't be falsified; the eternally living truth of his words has remained naked to me – unthinking at the time, but fully understood the instant it fixed itself in a corner of my memory, perhaps inseparable from the words that came with it.

To tell the truth, so as to adhere as closely as possible to the register of his vocabulary and his own expressions, I'd transcribed that crucial moment with extreme caution – concerned about how best I could convey its absolute accuracy – to the point of consulting the Battambang interviews[10] where Duch goes over his disgust during interrogations.

Nonetheless, Duch replied straying from the point in a way that was not typical of him, going back over the circumstances, associating the statements that I attributed to him with precise and isolated events,[11] or with his fatigue at the time and with malaria; the rest he no longer remembered well.

The magistrate pressed on:

'Do you think that what Mr Bizot reports does not correspond with what you said? Is it the truth, or not?'

The defendant stood up: 'Yes, I think what he described represents the exact truth.'

I would never get to the bottom of his answer: whatever his truth was, it was out of the question for him to contradict me publicly, at the risk of getting tripped up himself.

*

After a break, it was the prosecution's turn to question me. The judge gave the stand to the foreign assistant prosecutor.

'You were not beaten, all right . . . But what about the psychological torture, especially the defendant's *Ha! Ha! Ha!* jokes?'

Beyond the images of torture and death intermingling in my head in a nightmarish play, I had to give impromptu testimony about the 'pranks' that the defendant could amuse himself with, beginning with the most disconcerting one, the one he himself was still most embarrassed about.[12] That day when, scarcely having returned from the meeting where my fate had been decided – with the duly signed order for my liberation in his pocket – the young guerrilla had hidden his impatience to tell me the good news, walked over nonchalantly, and brusquely told me the opposite, taking on a serious look . . . just as a joke.

I understood right away where the prosecutor was heading. His role was to appease everyone, and for that he had to stick to the dogma: the *abnormality* and perversity of the criminal, the *inhumanity* of the torturer . . . even if it meant deforming the model at the cost of the likeness. He was willing to take a narrow view, to create reassuring symmetries, to drive him out of our own burrow: weird expressions, suspicious leanings, the habitus – floating the idea that Tuol Sleng was the work of a pervert, and the atrocities committed there the result of his predispositions. He meant to show that it couldn't have been done without him. Then, in front of fifteen plaintiffs, he'd go directly from the portrait to the caricature and pull out of his hat, like an apparition in a magic show, the final image of a snickering Jack the Ripper.

Of course, every major trial resorts to these sorts of confirmations, especially when the psychological evaluation has provided no reassuring conclusions; in the present case, the results were even so ordinary, so discouraging, that Duch's evaluation was the sort of thing that might be a cause of alarm for each and every one of us. Thus, given the need to put things back in their right place and protect our institutions – whether for themselves or for the public good – it fell to the prosecution to unearth psychological clues, even the most ordinary ones, that would implicate the defendant in a personal, physical, intimate way, in the crimes' process.

In truth, I complied all the more readily with the line of questioning since, by publicly performing his magic trick, the public official had unintentionally proved my point. At M-13 reason had not always stifled our need to laugh – one that perhaps only grew stronger as everyone's anxiety increased.

And, in my opinion, this need to joke, with the guards or even with the prisoners, was precisely the most distinct, but also the most tragic, proof of Duch's humanity.

*

Later in the day, time was reserved for the lawyers of the four groups of plaintiffs.

Question from the foreign assistant lawyer for Group 1:

'In the many interviews you've given to the media these past few months and years, there is a recurring line: "you have to try to see the human being behind the mask of the monster." And you apparently have succeeded in this, in relation to the defendant, and you see the man in him. Of course, this approach is yours, and we respect it. I just have one question about it. You were not only a victim of the defendant. You were imprisoned by an organisation, the Khmer Rouge, and of course you know what they went on to do to this country, a country that you love. Are you similarly disposed to see the man beyond the torturer in relation to the Khmer Rouge leaders still alive and awaiting trial, with whom you had no direct interaction? I am thinking particularly of Nuon Chea.[13] Do you also manage to see the man in him?'

. . . My heart skipped a beat. I'm not sure! I was suddenly unsettled by the surprise, and I felt unable to give any reply. A massive shock filled my brain, a black hole that forced me to go back in time, to reconstruct the evolution of what I had progressively thought since M-13, to revisit my thoughts from within, until I could grasp the first threads of that 'philosophy of the mask' that Duch one day placed in my hand, to make me realise the distress hidden in him, in me, in everyone . . . What about Nuon

Chea, the regime's second in command, the high-ranking head of security who gave Duch instructions over the phone – the devil par excellence? Yes – No? . . . Was he the same person?

'Yes, sir . . . ' but my affirmation hung over the room for a long time, and the lawyer finally sat down and thanked me for my reply.

Actually, I had replied instinctively, without being sure of its meaning and consequences, on the verge of perhaps contradicting myself, of being led astray into one of those traps of logic where I am easily caught whenever deductions or *trompe l'oeil* symmetries are concerned. I know now that I did indeed have to answer 'yes', to be in keeping with myself and my feelings. What's more, I could scarcely go wrong, since, ultimately, I'd asserted nothing that would have been dictated by my gratitude to Duch, any more than by my aversion to all the Khmer Rouge. Simply put, I had perhaps never thought of the whole story using Nuon Chea or Ta Mok as starting points. In this respect, the party leaders had no more excuses than Duch, but from another perspective, they didn't deserve any more hatred. The guilt of some joined the guilt of others, without clearing anyone. That said, like everyone, I found it normal that Duch, unlike his superiors still awaiting judgment, should have cleared without hesitation his own subordinates, since none of them could avoid obeying orders.

*

The other shock of the afternoon came with a request from the French lawyer for Group 3, phrased in pleasant words, to which it was hard for me not to accede.

'I will put aside the facts, since many questions have been

asked of you. It seems to me that the lofty view you took earlier, the distance you willingly adopt, authorises me to ask you about your feelings. Do you permit me to proceed in this way with you?'

His question was in two parts. I unwillingly omitted to answer the first part, which had to do with the sincerity of the remorse expressed by the defendant. For me, this obsession with authenticity is beside the point. This repeated need even seems suspicious to me, out of place, bizarrely outdated, and in a sense shocking considering the number of dead. Is it so hard to understand that evil has been fully accomplished, at its highest level, and that the torturer can thus sincerely want to appease his conscience with regrets that are all the more real since he has fallen so steeply and so far? What finally are we trying to achieve, since, in any case, as soon as the truth of his feelings is brought into the open, it scares us so much that we refuse to believe in it!

'When you left your companions, they said to you: "French comrade, don't forget us!" If Lay and Son were here today, what would they expect from this confrontation, what would they expect from this trial, and please understand me, beyond those two companions, what can all these plaintiffs expect today?'

At first I again had no reply to give. How could I set myself up as a spokesman for the dead? But all of a sudden, weight-lessly in the court, the hordes of ghosts of M-13 came to my rescue; the fury I saw devouring Lay's heart awoke in me; the anguish I saw freeze Son's blood; the vengeance I saw convulse and blanch all the others. So with the words that they had breathed in my ear I spoke, immediately making myself their interpreter, to ask that the punishment of the torturer be precisely calculated to equal the suffering they themselves had endured.[14]

*

On 26 November, 2009, the final day of a trial that lasted almost two years, throughout which the prisoner did whatever he could in the service of the truth – cooperating, abandoning his right to silence, paving the way for the discovery of evidence, testifying against his former leaders, crying out his guilt and responsibility, acknowledging his cowardliness, asking forgiveness – Duch little by little stopped looking at the assistant prosecutors attentively, retreated into his shell, refused to answer questions that in any case had already been asked a hundred times, and in a general way, decided to fall silent once and for all, to stop listening, to turn his back on the rest of the world.[15]

*

The French assistant lawyer for the defence, François Roux:

'Mr Prosecutor, you have missed your appointment with history! [. . .] You have made a stock indictment whose implication is none other than: "This man is a monster, lock him up for forty years, and everything will be better in society!" Those words are hackneyed. We have to go further than that. We have to try to understand the mechanisms that make a man – a good man in every respect, as we say – one day become a torturer. That is what I would have liked to hear you discuss! Because, in the Nuremberg trial, they said the same thing: "These Nazi people are monsters. We will condemn them to death, and that will serve as an example." But after Nuremberg, Cambodia happened, Rwanda happened . . . What is this exemplarity, with its deterrent nature, you are looking for? What purpose does it serve in your conventional speeches, so long as you don't confront the real problem?'[16]

*

The prosecution had in fact played its role to perfection: in the name of society, the prosecutors managed to spread a feeling of permanent frustration, acting every day in such a way that the acknowledged facts seemed truncated, that the defendant's confessions seemed to hide from us the brutal, distressing aspect of reality. Public opinion rushed to this conviction of the magistrates, the way one rushes to look for help: 'Duch wasn't saying everything'; his remorse was not expressed directly or sincerely. End of discussion. From the beginning, everything had been done to make us understand that *he* was the guilty one, that individual, precisely; and that this had nothing to do with 'humanity'. Duch was the one the law was punishing. He deserved the maximum sentence that could be handed down to him by the law of the people, without the crux of the problem being dealt with, or ever mentioned.

Duch knew the price, he knew his inexpiable crime, and did not try to flee: 'The best I can do is to kneel down and beg forgiveness. The victims and the survivors can point their fingers at me. I am not offended by that. It is their right and I accept it respectfully. Even if the people stone me to death, I won't say anything, I won't say I'm disappointed or that I want to kill myself. I am responsible for my actions and it's everyone's free choice whether or not to forgive me. I am here to accept my responsibility. I am full of remorse for what I've done, and I speak from the bottom of my heart. I am not on any account using that as an excuse. My words are sincere'.[17]

Nothing could soothe Duch any longer, except for one thing: his collaboration with the law had been intended to show, as naively, as correctly, as sincerely as possible, how important it was that he be heard and believed. He found that he had the courage to endure any pain – in line with his regrets – in his own name, as one who repents for his own crimes. But his effigy, turned crude caricature, had already been pinned in place: with shrill screams, we look at the mask of the monster so as not to make out the familiar face of a human being.

That was asking the impossible.

So the torturer fell silent, in keeping with what was expected of him. Then finally, he asked for the termination of the proceedings, as if lowering his arms, in a turnabout that stemmed from more than the political pressure exercised by his Cambodian lawyer, whose goal was to attune his defence with that of his former leaders, whose trial was beginning.[18] This change was a reaction to the basic deafness of the Office of Assistant Prosecutors, itself echoing a far more primal autism: our inability to hear at once whatever is odious and whatever is pitiful in human nature.

Beyond Tuol Sleng's walls, there is nothing that refers us to anything but ourselves.[19] Will we ever have the courage to acquire this vision and to admit it to ourselves? Shall we become aware that we devour and fight not only others but ourselves, that we destroy and self-destroy, and have done ever since we committed the original betrayal in order to become masters of the living world?

The evils we endure go back to 'a deeper, wider abyss [than our past], they seem prior to our birth'.[20]

*

Human pride has been left safe by this trial: the monster has not been identified. Duch no longer scares us. But how much is there to fear from the torturer's silence – this silence about ourselves that echoes my mother's silence from long ago – as if everything were already complete in our innermost selves . . .[21]

Postscript

Duch now feels cheated by everyone, perhaps by me too. Not because I set myself up against him and spoke for the dead – that I know he understands – but because I put him on a par with the worst of the leaders whose orders he carried out, Nuon Chea, the cold and remorseless man, author of Duch's misfortune and object of his anger: the only one after Pol Pot to whom he thought he would never be compared.

PART TWO

DOCUMENT 1:

Miscellaneous on *The Gate* by François Bizot

[by Kaing Guek Eav, aka Duch]

The Gate was only given to Duch after his transfer to a new prison. I asked him to read it, and to note as he went the impressions that this return to events of the past evoked in him – like the new thoughts that might be shaped by rubbing shoulders with my own.

The following text is the result of Duch's reading. He sent it to me in 2008, on six double-sided pages covered in his careful handwriting. I have respected here the same line breaks, parentheses and notes as in the original letter.

Introduction

For a long time now, I just have to recall [the name of] *lok*[1] Bizot for very refreshing memories to come to mind. He was the one who told me: 'The vowels and consonants of the Khmer alphabet are an expression of the virtues of the mother and father.'[2] That is one of the things I remember.

Usually, I feel great pity for him, especially when I remember making that inappropriate joke, and his whole body shuddered, so that he almost fainted and fell to his knees. Actually, the reason he made me joke that way with him came from my excitement about knowing that Pol Pot was freeing Bizot, despite the refusals of Ta Mok, whose base heart could do nothing more.

Also, when I remember the case of *lok* Bizot, I myself feel the boundless remorse that haunts him for not having been able to save Lay and Son.

The different points on which I would like to dwell now do not directly concern *lok* Bizot, or Lay, or Son, but the crimes that were committed by the Kampuchea Communist Party (KCP), which I belonged to, and whose criminal orders I carried out to the best of my ability at M-13.

1. My burden

At the time when I knew *lok* Bizot, the difficulties I had been accumulating since 1964 had grown much heavier. It was the weight of the hell fires that I mistook at the time for the fires of a diamond . . . My burden is the total faith I placed in the KCP, because I regarded it as the vital spirit of the people and the Khmer nation. I devoted my life and my personal fate to the Party. I entrusted it with the care of guiding me, teaching me, with no restriction whatsoever. I was one of its most ardent supporters.

2. The situation in the liberated zone at the end of 1971

a) The great disagreement that set us against the North Vietnamese (who had suddenly become our enemies, because they were seizing every opportunity to take hold of large portions of Khmer territory to govern in place of us), eventually died down. They decided to withdraw from the regions they had coveted, like Kien Svay, Sa Ang, Koh Thom, Leuk Dek, and to camp only on our lands as guests.

b) In the Southwest Region, major class disagreements also appeared between the high-ranking officials:

—As early as 1968, Ta Mok opposed the influence of intellectual cadres [in the Party], and over a period of 24 hours, four of them were expelled from the Southwest Region.*

—Ta Mok stubbornly refused them the slightest military responsibility, and managed to restrict their actions to the levels of villages, districts and provinces.

—It was only in the middle of 1971 that Pol Pot decided to join together the region's intellectual cadres to create a 'special zone'. M-13 was born then – on 20 July 1971.

3. Reflections on the situation

I would like to give my opinion on the actual situation, during these different periods, at the end of 1971.

*Khet Pen, aka Sou, a university professor; Kè Kem Huot, aka Mon, a university professor; Chea Houn, aka Van, a high-school professor; Oum Chheun aka Mai, a high-school professor. These four people were squashed after 17 April. [*Duch's note*]

The way the Party went about settling the dispute that opposed us to the North Vietnamese had the effect of immediately reinforcing my admiration and faith in the Party.

In fact, like most intellectual cadres I thought that it had once and for all put an end to the rivalries that had flared up among the leadership, especially in Sa Ang, Koh Thom, Leuk Dek, Kien Svay, and that that would never be able to happen again. Who would have believed that Pol Pot and Ta Mok were in the process of preparing a plan to kill everyone, and thus to extend their power into all domains throughout the country? Chay Kim Huor[3] thought that Ta Mok's oppression was still acceptable and that it was going in the right direction. I myself agreed, and thought the same thing.

But these differences of opinion on a national level (at that time, I still refused to talk about disputes between enemies) were leading more and more, against all laws, to the arrest and imprisonment of people. Many times, Von Veth[4] and Chay Kim Huor came to explain to me that, in history's eyes, it was the one who ordered the arrest and imprisonment who would have to answer for it, without a shadow of a doubt. The order came from members of the Central Committee, for instance from Bang Bal (aka Huot Heng), secretary of Zone 32, but also a longtime member of the Central Committee. At any rate, it should be understood that we were fighting to free the nation, that is, to free the population, the people, not to free the nation without the people.

It was because of my blind optimism about the KCP that I was unable to evaluate the situation correctly.

4. Pol Pot's position toward the French government

According to my own observations and analyses, I think Pol Pot strongly felt the need to be recognised by the government of France.

Therefore, before 17 April 1975, the considerations that impacted on his wish to see the French recognise the 'United National Front of Kampuchea' (UNFK) were the following:

—The liberation of François Bizot;
—The invitation of the journalist Serge Thion,[5] to the freed regions of the 'special zone';
—Finally, the anger** he felt against Groslier.[6]

After 17 April 1975 (and from what I remember, during a political meeting that took place in 1977):

—Son Sen gave the order to the troops billeted in the French Embassy, to clean the site quickly, probably in view of an impending reinstatement of diplomatic relations [with France].

**I do not know what reasons there were behind Pol Pot's anger towards Groslier. But I remember that at a meeting for the 'special zone's' intellectual leaders, just before the debate, Hou Youn had sent Phok Chhay to ask me: 'Why release Bizot?' I replied: 'Comrade Pol Pot decided so.' Thereafter, in his first speech, Hou Youn did not hesitate to call Groslier a 'thug'. It was clear that this insult came from the fact that Pol Pot was indignant with Groslier, and that Groslier must have done something. The relationship between Pol Pot and the French finally followed this path. In 1990, Pol Pot became furious with the French and said: 'Just wait until things fall into place!' (In other words, 'until I share power with Hun Sen'). 'I will eliminate French classes from all of Kampuchea's schools'.

—It was on this occasion that he let it be known that in a
   French newspaper (I've forgotten the name of the paper)
   the situation was reported in a positive way.*** It was stated
   that Phnom Penh remained calm. I was facing him at this
   moment, and he repeated [in French]: a 'majestic silence'.

All this leads me to think that Pol Pot counted on France so
as not to remain alone, and to protect himself from the attacks
that were coming from all sides. In so doing, he had placed
himself so high that no one was able to extend a hand to him
any more.

5. The criminal arrest of François Bizot is a political hostage-taking

To say that it was a hostage-taking is not something I could
express at the time.

At that time, I knew that [the monastery of] Vat O was in a
zone under the control [of the soldiers] of Lon Nol, and that
the [Khmer Rouge] militia, which was under the command of
Comrade Rom (leader of the militia of Ponhea Leu), had come
upon a Frenchman and two Cambodians there. I deduced they
hadn't intended to penetrate into the liberated zone under our
control. In these conditions, I tried to protect all three of them.
None of them were from the CIA; they weren't spying on
anything at all. That said, I was still somewhat careful, and I did

***Son Sen was glad about this, in his wish for a flattering image of the KCP
to be spread throughout the world.

not ask right away for their release, as I had already done on other occasions and as I would do again.

Later on, I understood that it was a hostage-taking for the following reasons:

—Pol Pot knew perfectly well that the Angkor Conservation
   was not [a spy lair].
—Pol Pot knew the [generally favourable] attitude of the
   French towards him and [their quite opposite attitude]
   towards Lon Nol.
—Pol Pot knew better than anyone how much he needed the
   French to support his cause.

Pol Pot had immediately been informed by Von Veth of the arrest of these three people from the Angkor Conservation, one of whom was a Frenchman. He had them imprisoned separately for months, so as to frighten them and sadden them.[†] Then at the instant of freeing them, he arrogantly decided to release the Frenchman alone, and to keep the two Khmers.

Who can dare make such a decision? Who can accept it? No one. No one would agree to it.

By ordering Chay Kim Hor to give François Bizot a copy of the Political Programme of the UNFK and some propaganda photos, and to explain the political situation to him, Pol Pot simply compromised himself [with the French].

[†]Actually, this affair was not up to Von Veth alone, and that's why I didn't dare ask for their release right away.

6. About the liberation by Pol Pot of François Bizot, Lay and Son.

Pol Pot refused to release Lay and Son, and decided to leave them with me. The decision immediately gave me a start, but I could do nothing else. At first I was afraid; then I saw that Ta Mok preferred to 'keep his tail low' in front of me.

It should be pointed out that Ta Mok had always found good reasons to oppose *lok* Bizot's release. For instance, he said: 'We are in the field, we see [things] more clearly [than above].' But in these cases, Von Veth answered him with one phrase: 'That Frenchman, it's wrong; he's not from the CIA!' Then Ta Mok would immediately switch and say: 'Release him, Comrade Duch! Release him!'

It was during such discussions that I realised that Ta Mok was smaller than Von Veth.

In 1976, I also understood that each decision from the General Party Secretary [Pol Pot] had to be applied without discussion, without bargaining.

In the case of *lok* Bizot, there was never any agreement between me and what Ta Mok wanted. That said, I did not think that Ta Mok was really angry or upset with me, since his behaviour could change very quickly. I thought there were no deep conflicts between us.

Back to the business of Lay and Son, when Pol Pot decided to keep them near me.

It would be wrong to suppose that I did not understand the suffering it was for them to remain separated from their wives, separated from their children. Obviously I understood that! But I did not have the power to help reunite them with their families. In my view, there was only one way [to help them, aside from freeing them]: to sympathise, to feel affection for them, to protect them, to regard them as brothers, as partisans of the group. I personally had the hope, and even the conviction, that I would manage to protect them until they found their people again, once the country was liberated. The promise I made was absolutely sincere at that time.

What's more, I also felt great pity for *lok* Bizot, when he left alone, leaving Lay and Son with me. His face was drawn. [I remember that] he walked from one side to the other, first to Lay, then to Son, then to all three together . . . It was painful to observe, but I could do nothing about it.

7. The organisation of M-13 in 1972

Some time after *lok* Bizot's departure:

—I moved the Office 13 to Tuol Svay Meas, on one side of Mount Pis, so that the place where we were going to set up would be sunny and at the same time far from habitation. There were rice paddies. The interrogations were placed under the responsibility of Comrade Pon, security under that of Comrade Meas.
—I left Lay and Son in Phum Prek, to work in the rice paddy with Comrade Net.

(I should point out that Net lived in Phum Kok. But after an argument with Ta Mok, he had wanted to come with me. At that time, I was more foolhardy, and I agreed to take him.)
    Thereafter:

I suggested to Von Veth that a branch of Office 13 be created, reserved for common people who had had a problem (without tying them up or questioning them). Only to strengthen them for a brief period before releasing them. He agreed. This branch was named M-13b, near Phum Sdok Srat, a commune of Sdok Tol, district of Ang Snuol. Comrade Soum, the former Vice President of M-13,[7] became President of M-13b. Then I charged Comrade Phal, member of the Communist Youth of Kampuchea, to become Comrade Soum's second in command.

I finally asked Von Veth for authorisation to send Lay and Son to Comrade Soum, but he refused. He thought they should stay a while longer to work in the rice paddy.

8. The rebellion at M-13a

Phum Prek became a section of the branch of Office 13, called M-13a, in Tuol Svay Meas. I liked to go there to meditate, and sometimes I managed to calm my soul.

Not long afterwards, Von Veth decided to assign four hardened fighters to Phum Prek: Samnang, Cheang, Piseth, and Raksmey, all from Zone 25, behind their leader Sien San. This brought the number of forces there to seven people [counting Lay and Son].

One day, around five in the afternoon, one of the fighters from Tuol Svay Meas came running to Phum Prek to tell me: 'The enemy got hold of our rifles and shot at us! All [the prisoners] have escaped!' I immediately ordered Comrade Samnang to go and help [the wounded], then Comrade Net to stand guard in the village. I had to warn Von Veth, and I went to ask the leader of Omleang to take me by motorbike.

We arrived on site at around seven o'clock. Night had fallen. I asked the liaison office agent to announce my arrival. Von Veth immediately told me: 'In the Southwest, they opened a camp for fighters, the place is near you. Did they come to your aid?' I answered 'No.' He got angry: 'Comrade, I think you've shown yourself quite careless! The enemy had a plan and you noticed nothing!'

The next week, I returned to see him again. He received me in the usual way, his mood was normal. The time seemed propitious for me to apologise to him and to ask for a strict application of the rules, with the ensuing punishment. Von Veth looked at me, his face hardened, then he turned away, motionless, without uttering a word . . . He never spoke to me again about that affair.

[Following the prisoners' escape] I abandoned Tuol Svay Meas and everyone returned to Phum Prek. I thought we would stay there just to work in the rice paddy, without ever changing. But who could think of only working in the rice paddy? Quickly, they brought other victims for me to interrogate.

Life forces us to do things we do not like doing . . . we can rarely avoid hurting ourselves.

At that moment, I couldn't help thinking about the poem 'The Death of the Wolf', by Alfred de Vigny.

9. The disagreement between Ta Mok and me

I am someone who tries naturally not to listen to gossip, which comes from everywhere, even though it's hard to avoid hearing it. Ta Mok had a particular knack for getting into arguments with intellectuals.

As far as I was concerned, I did everything to be in contact with him as little as possible, but no matter what, I remained his target because of [the help I had imprudently given to] Comrade Net. Forewarned, I did my best to make no more mistakes.

The criminal decision, which he made then at M-13, concerning the case of Jacques Loiseleur,[8] holds a hidden truth for me: it shows very clearly that he was still very angry with me. Ta Mok warned me right away: 'This time, don't try to make yourself a lawyer for another Frenchman and ask for his liberation again!'

10. The crime against the seven people at M-13 in Phum Prek

In 1973, I saw Von Veth again, who had just returned from a workshop with high-ranking people. That night, we both sat on the trunk of a dead tree lying near his house. He asked me for news of the general situation, as well as of the seven people assigned to the rice paddies in Phum Prek. In the end, he said to me: 'We have to "resolve" the case of the 7 people:

'Next time, [you'll know that one] must never vouch for people who have a history as spies, much less have them enter the ranks of the Party.

'Comrade, above all do not forget that you have Chinese

blood! The Chinese Communist Party is indeed very powerful, but among the many Chinese foreigners [in Cambodia], the Party trusts only Ta Hong,[††] because he is the only one we have known for a long time.

'Moreover, comrade: Ta Mok denounced you to the Central Committee. He doesn't want you here any more.'

Instantly I felt great fear.

Concerning the fate of the seven people, I begged him, using the excuse that Raksmi's sister, who lived in Ang Snuol, had come, with her husband (a very well known former head of a pagoda), to visit her brother in Phum Prek. These seven people had been living in the free zone for a long time. If we had now to 'resolve' [the seven cases], that would not fail to cause a sensation. Von Veth remained silent for a while, then ordered the following: 'Considering that the forces you have at your command are few and made up of young people, let's leave the fighters in the Southwest Region to decide it themselves. I will speak to them.'

I never tried again to understand [anything] about that day, nor why our Party had ordered the death of these [seven] people.

11. Concerning the interrogations

Starting from that time, I devoted myself completely to my job as interrogator. Then, as the days went by, I let myself be convinced that [the issue of] my transfer had been suspended.

[††] Nget You, aka Hong, whom the Party decided to arrest and send to S-21 on 13 March, 1978. This decision was one of the first signs that made me fear for my life.

My first experience [as interrogator]

One day I had to question people suspected of hiding a stash of rifles, and got nowhere. My chiefs had promised me that, if it came to that, they would take full responsibility in the eyes of history for the orders [to torture] that I had received. Immediately, I chided myself for having acted too timidly, thinking all the while that I had a personality very poorly suited for this sort of task. I thought about it for a long time, turning the problem over in my head.

My second experience [as interrogator]

That time I had to interrogate someone named Nget Sombon, better known under the name he used as a writer: Rompé. From his [forced] confessions, I deduced the following lessons:

—His confession could only be 50 per cent true.
—The names of the accomplices he denounced (Pol Pot was extremely interested in this) could only be 30 per cent true.
—The network that was the basis of his organisation's agents was completely wrong.

My theory on interrogations

I refer to Sun Tzu, the Chinese military theoretician, when he said: 'If you know the enemy and know yourself you need not fear the outcome of a hundred battles.' Because I understood that: interrogation is a fight that is played out between an interrogator and the one who must reply; from one to the other. Each one is looking for the weak point in his opponent, in a confrontation where each opposes the other.

In this way, you could say that [the kind] of interrogation that *lok* Bizot underwent under Comrade Nuon[†††] deserved the name 'Revealing his weak points': Bizot grasped this immediately – p. 36, *The Gate*. Comrade Nuon does not yet know who François Bizot is, when he lies and states he had seen him on the streets of Prei Nokor (Saigon). He didn't have to say one word more to convince the suspect that the interrogator knew nothing at all.

Allow me to recall the two points that I taught comrades in charge of interrogating [prisoners]:

—Before asking a question, you should prepare carefully.
—Concerning the one being interrogated who guesses our
    intentions. If you already know what you want a suspect to
    answer, his reply will always be in keeping with your
    request. That is the greatest error of interrogators, and
    precisely the mistake that should be avoided.

The interrogation

Necessary as it may be, [interrogation] is only a small part of police work. The confessions we obtain thus can't contain more than 20 or 30 per cent of the truth. The KCP knew that. Confessions were always evaluated and understood according to this principle: 'Before cutting down bamboo, you must first clear away the thorns.'

[†††] Nuon, whose first name was Prasat, is the younger brother of Ta Prasith, aka Chong. Nuon was trained in Hanoi from 1954 to 1970. When he met François Bizot, he was commanding the troops of the Southwest Region.

The multitude of crimes of all sorts committed against humanity by the KCP, against the Cambodian people, actually began in 1970. The action in M-13 entered into this framework on 20 July 1971. As President of M-13, I sincerely accept full responsibility for all the crimes that were perpetrated there, for which I have the most painful remorse.

Conclusion

> At the same time, I felt deep guilt about my two companions; I was suddenly aware that I should also reassure their own families and support them.
>
> The Gate, p. 122

The words above have great power; they made me realise and become aware that, in the past, I did not realise the extent of the state of chronic suffering that already deeply affected *lok* Bizot.

May God forgive his child, this child who was not able to measure the suffering of his victim, François Bizot!

May God have pity, grant his protection, and give prosperity to *lok* Bizot!

May God have pity on the souls of Lay and Son; may he forgive *lok* Bizot; may he forgive his child, in his mercy.

Then I acknowledged my sin to you
and did not cover up my iniquity.
I said, 'I will confess
my transgressions to the LORD.'
And you forgave
the guilt of my sin.

Psalm 32: 5

DOCUMENT 2:

Deposition of Mr François Bizot Witness for the Court No. 1

(8–9 April 2009)

The text that follows is the transcript of my deposition before the Extraordinary Chambers of the Courts of Cambodia in Phnom Penh on 8 and 9 April 2009. It also includes the most salient moments of my questioning over the same two days by the prosecutors, judges and lawyers, both for the accused and the civil plaintiffs.

PRESIDING JUDGE:

'The court is now open. Let the bailiff bring in the witness.

'Mr François Bizot, can you describe what you saw in the Security Camp M-13, during your detention, and until your liberation and return to Phnom Penh?'

WITNESS:

'Certainly, Your Honour. [. . .] My research on Cambodian Buddhism brought me to the Udong region, having been

chased out of Angkor's Reservation and Park where I lived and worked until the North Vietnamese invasion. I continued my research in the Kandal Province. On 10 October 1971, I left for north of Udong to visit the monastery of Vat O, near the village of Tuol Tophi. I was in a car belonging to the French School of the Far East, with my daughter Hélène who was not yet three, the two co-workers whose names I have mentioned, and accompanied by two or three people from the village who were showing me the way. Having arrived at Vat O, we were received by the Venerable Abbot, and I realised that things weren't going at all as planned; the Abbot was very nervous. That's when I realised that either an ambush had been set up for us, or that we had unluckily fallen upon a militia patrol. I was immediately apprehended and my two co-workers were tied up, arms behind their backs. I fought and refused to be tied up, and I was brought, at my request – or so I thought – to meet the leader, in the village of Tuol Tophi. We stayed there for almost two hours. During those two hours, I was questioned by a leader, who listened to what I had to say, especially that I was coming to this monastery to study the rituals of Cambodian Buddhism, and at the end of my explanations, he deduced that I was a CIA agent and told me so. My armpits were searched, perhaps for a microphone. I don't know. Then my two comrades were taken away from me, and I was tied up and led along a country path under the surveillance of two young guards, one of whom held a rifle.

'I spent the first night in a sort of room next to a few huts, and then the next morning I arrived at a village that I didn't recognise. My two companions were there already, upstairs in a house where there was a massive yoke made of wood, a *knoh*, between whose beams their legs were locked in half-moon openings. I took my place next to them, lying on my back in the same position. Some time afterwards, they came to get me in order to try me before a tribunal made up of a Kraum Khmer soldier, recognisable from his accent, acting as judge, flanked by two clerks who noted down what I said. There were about fifty villagers around us. Leaning on a table set up on a platform, the inquisitor told me he knew me, that he had seen me in Saigon, and that the lackeys of American imperialism needed people like me, who spoke the Khmer language, to pay the fighters in the service of the Americans, because they didn't trust their own soldiers. I obviously denied this accusation, which made no sense to me – adding that if he was already certain of my guilt, he would have to kill me without delay. My remark immediately provoked applause from the public behind me. Then – if you will allow me to shorten things a little, especially since I no longer remember the details very well – but the judge said that there were contradictions between what the Angkar knew and what I had just said. So I had to be regarded as someone who was in the position of being accused of something that he did not acknowledge. Immediately I was put back in the yoke. A meal was served to us. Then, after hearing shouts around the house of "What are you waiting for? Strip and kill him!" the Khmer soldiers came upstairs, took me out alone, blindfolded my eyes, and I was led away to be executed.

'I will never know if it was a mock-execution or an order that was not carried out. Whatever the case, I remained alive and was pushed on to a path that was to lead me, from stage to stage, to M-13 the next morning. It turned out that Lay and Son were already there, or arrived soon after me. I didn't have an overall view of the camp right away, and I was received by a leader who seemed immediately cynical and aggressive. He gave the necessary orders for one of my ankles to be placed in shackles at the end of a common rail to which fifteen or twenty detainees were already fettered. They had no room, and I was frightened not just by the principle of the shackle but also by the situation I would occupy at the end of the chain. Since I have thick bones, my ankle wouldn't go through the opening. The leader ordered a larger shackle to be found.

'Then a young man arrived, whose presence I hadn't noticed right away, just when I was asking permission to go and wash in the river. I had walked for two days and two nights on dusty paths in the rain and I was covered in mud. It was at that moment, when I was insisting on going to wash myself, that the young man who came over intervened to give me permission. I understood then that the leader of the camp was not the aggressive man who had received me, but that this man was a leader, able to contradict him – excuse me Your Honour, I forgot to point out that the prisoners were not on any account allowed to bathe. So I went to wash myself. When I came back, since the problem of the shackles hadn't been resolved, the young man himself gave the order that I be put in a separate place, outside of the perimeter of the three barracks reserved for the prisoners – about forty of them, between forty and fifty. I was led to a sheltered place which had a bamboo hut meant for storing the three or four bags of rice that the villagers from the region brought to the camp every week in a cart. So the place was already full with the bags that were there. I was chained by the foot beneath this sort of awning, and I remember that the rain began to fall. Evening came; a meal was served to me by one of the young guards who had to jump between the pools of water. That was my first night in the camp, and I soon fell asleep.

'The next day, I became better acquainted with the man I had realised was the leader of the camp, whose name I learned from the guards was Duch. They called him Ta Duch when they spoke of him. He decided to conduct the interrogations himself. He told me there were charges against me, which were very serious, and I had to write my first declaration of innocence. I wrote a number of declarations of innocence on pieces of paper that he gave me himself, with much emotion each time, because I thought it would be a part of the things I would leave behind me, probably the last. The feel of the camp very soon seemed that of a place you didn't get out of alive. The young guards on whom every instant of my daily existence depended spoke among themselves, with the childishness and also perverseness of their age, and it was easy to guess what they were talking about and what I had to expect, along with my fellow inmates.

'That being the case, the interrogations went on every day, between the leader and me. He was twenty-seven, I was thirty. Under the fire of his questions, even though they were always asked with a certain amount of amiability I should say, and because of the permanent anger I had at being taken for something I wasn't – at this injustice that consisted of taking me for a CIA spy, whereas those things were so far from my mind – I was led to rebel and ask him questions in return; and this lasted for weeks and weeks. It is obvious that at that pace, a certain habit was created between us, which wove certain ties of regular contact. If I remember correctly, Duch had to write up a report at least every week. I saw him writing very late at night and very early in the morning. His reputation was that of an indefatigable worker who spoke little and was deeply invested in his responsibilities as camp leader. My interrogations were always conducted politely and I was never beaten.

'I think Duch thought that if I was a CIA agent, the best way in any case to get the truth from me would probably not be to hit me, but to engage in conversation with me, and the way to break through to me was to ask me questions about my work, my activities at the Angkor Conservation Centre, about Cambodian Buddhism, which he was less familiar with than I was, and he requested that I give as many details as I could, with the aim, apparently, of checking if I did in fact have the profile of a researcher or the abilities required to work on the history, inscriptions and texts of Cambodian Buddhism.

'I asked Duch for a notebook, which he brought me one day, along with a Bic pen and a razor blade. I really wanted to have a shave. Your Honour, I kept that notebook. I could perhaps show you the cover and a few pages right now[1]. [. . .] I just want to show this evidence, the notebook that Duch brought me, which I filled with childhood memories, some poems; I tried to write a persuasive argument in it about my researches into Buddhism, to show that I was in fact a researcher. Later on, when it turned out that I was going to be freed, I asked Duch if I could keep this notebook with me, and he was anxious to examine it himself before deciding. He read it, I think with great care, asked me a few questions in the meantime, then returned it to me. So it's still with me. I should say that this notebook, which I brought back with me, I have never reread.

'Duch came back, as I've said, at least once a week, from the village or wherever it was he seemed to have to go. It was striking to see in what poor health Duch seemed to be, like most of us. Well, I shouldn't really say "us", since chance willed it that I was never ill, so much so that I was embarrassed. When people asked me questions about the state of my health, I made up a few headaches so as not to arouse their jealousy. It was in October, November, December, and as you know, Your Honour, that's the period for malaria, and the ravages of malaria in the camp caused many deaths. The ones who didn't die of it suffered greatly from fatigue. One day, Duch told me he was going to leave the next day and he might have good news to tell me when he returned. So I was very impatient for him to return, and it was after his reappearance that he was able to let me know that I would be able to rejoin my family. When I heard this news, which I didn't believe right away – I should say, Your Honour, that nothing was said; lies were the oxygen we breathed, and we all breathed out this bad oxygen from our chests. Lies were present too when someone was led to his death: he was never told; it was denied until the last instant. So I had difficulty believing in this promise of freedom. As I have pointed out, I could never show proof of my non-guilt, and Duch himself would never have any of my guilt. I at least was the only one to believe in it. That being the case, hope never leaves the prisoner. And at the same time I had already understood that my life depended on him, that my existence was in his hands; not in mine alone.

'When he told me I was going to be set free, it was news that I did not react to with the joy one should expect, and my answer, my attitude was to say: "So prove it! Take off these chains!" Those chains which I found so painful. Duch immediately gave the order to the young guards, who took off my chains. Then I said right away: "If I am freed, I am innocent. And if I am innocent, the two Khmers who are with me are too, so free them!" Duch gave the orders to the young guards for my two companions to be untied. So I saw them again after three months. Needless to say, this reunion was incredibly important to us although we didn't show it openly – we didn't even talk much. This gave me reason to hope. The same could not be said for Lay and Son. They thought it was a way to make them swallow the pill. And not one of them, not one of my fellow inmates, thought when they saw me leave that I would be freed. They all secretly thought that the path they were going to make me take was also the one that my predecessors had followed.

'I was to be set free, then, on Christmas Day. Because of a stupid fuss about a motorbike which had been taken by a guard and not brought back on time, my liberation was delayed till the next day. Obviously, this delay in the schedule was very unsettling. But whatever the case it was Christmas night, and this was the chance, since I was free, to spend my first night without chains, but also to get to know better, let's say from a different perspective, or to see differently, someone who would also have a different attitude to me, since I was in a situation that was almost . . . not even intermediary, since I was in the process of being freed. And, around a fire that the guards often lit at night, because it was cold – and I should say that the cold, at that time of the year, in the Cardamom forest, was particularly keen, the nights icy – I took advantage during the coldest nights of a burning log that the guards brought me so the ground I slept on wouldn't be so cold.

'So I went over to the fire where Duch would be, I've forgotten the details, and this was an opportunity to speak. We spoke more freely, about our families, but Duch as far as I know didn't have any, apart from his parents . . . I mean that he wasn't himself the head of a family, he had no children at the time. And Duch was also interested in hearing what had become of Hélène, my little girl who had accompanied me in the car and who had remained in the last village, before Vat O, with one of the girls who had also come with us. And I confess that this circumstance was at the origin of the constant suffering I felt throughout my entire detention, not knowing where she might be or what had become of her. Duch tried to reassure me about this.

'I had had, a few days before, on two occasions, the opportunity to question myself on the means the camp employed to make prisoners talk. For I had understood, still without . . . by interpreting signs and messages, essentially from the guards – which, despite the orders they had received, told me practically everything: I knew that we were not far from Omleang, they spoke about it amongst themselves – I understood that the prisoners were beaten. The authorisation to wash myself on the first day was renewed, and I was permitted to take a bath every night. During one of my bathing sessions, in a river that wasn't more than thirty centimetres deep but was at least a freshwater river, I climbed the opposite bank, a few dozen metres high, and I saw a hut that I went over to. I saw that it housed a bamboo horizontal bar that was quite thick, with sliding rattan rings, obviously meant to hold someone by the wrists. I quickly went back but I remembered this.

'And another memory, still returning from my washing. This was for me the only occasion when I was able to have a different view of the camp from the one afforded solely by the length of my chain. I fell on one of the prisoners who seemingly had been imprisoned long enough to be authorised to walk around in the camp, while still bound by the same fate as the others. He was sharpening a rattan stick. Passing near him, I said to him, "Hey, comrade! Who are you going to hit with that rod?" The unhappy man looked at me, crying out that he wasn't the one who was going to do the hitting. Actually I was joking, since I was far from imagining that he was in fact whittling a rod.

'So it wasn't with any real certainty, just a series of deductions, that on Christmas Eve I asked Duch: "But who is it that does the hitting?" Duch didn't hesitate to answer me that he sometimes hit the prisoners, whenever they lied, and when their statements contradicted each other. That he couldn't bear lies. That this work made him . . . I don't remember the precise words but maybe that this work made him vomit. But that it was his responsibility, that it was what the Angkar expected of him. This work corresponded to his duties. I was terrified. And I think that this episode, which was for me a fundamental event, is at the origin of a long process which took place in me. . . .

'I can say, Your Honour, that until then I'd felt safe. I thought I was on the right side of humanity and that there were monsters I could never resemble, thank God, and that there was a difference – in history, in sensibility – that it was a state of nature, that not everyone could be that way. That some were born like that, and that others would never be that way. I have to say that Duch's reply, in light of what I had learned of him over the course of the interrogations, made the scales fall from my eyes. That Christmas Eve, when I was waiting, when he told me that, to discover a monster, "inhuman" as we are used to saying, I realised that it was infinitely more tragic, infinitely more terrifying, and that I had opposite me a man who resembled many of my friends: a Marxist, a communist Marxist, who was close to giving his life if he had to for his country, for the revolution in which he believed, and that the ultimate aim of this engagement was the well-being of the inhabitants of Cambodia, a struggle against injustice, and, even if these were clichés used to describe the Khmer peasantry, from which the communist Cambodian revolution was nourished, this land without the Khmer, which was portrayed as an archetype that had been made from whole cloth, but even if there was a diabolical naivety in this archetype, there was also a basic sincerity, probably on his part as well as among many revolutionaries – and I myself had at the time in Paris friends who were perfectly engaged in this communist revolution and who looked at what was happening in Cambodia with an eye that revolted me, but which was also justified in their opinion by an end that justified the means. This end that justified the means being the independence of Cambodia, its right to self-determination, and then the end of poverty – dreams, finally, but the Cambodians weren't the first men in history to kill to make their dreams come true.

'So I saw, for the first time, behind the mask worn by the monster opposite me. It was also his duty to interrogate prisoners. I didn't see everything – far from it but I can only bear witness in terms of what I understood and the memories I have of it. So his work was to write up reports about the people who were sent to him to be executed. I realised then, that the monster in question had human qualities that were disturbing and frightening, and that from then on I too was no longer safe from that, that we were all no longer safe. And that the worst would certainly be to make these monsters into special people. So it was much more complicated than that.

'I didn't phrase everything that way at the time. But it was this meeting, this ordeal from which I didn't think I'd emerge alive, that was at the source of a sort of simmering, and that, the day I learned that Duch was still alive, rose up again. For I thought that if there was one thing to say, it was that . . . Especially since in the meantime the horror of the crimes of Tuol Sleng was added to the gravity of the events at M-13 – and thus if there was one thing to say it is that I had met a young man, at the time when he was a budding revolutionary, who had progressively received, under the gaze of his people, a mission, which he acquitted himself of in a frightening way but with great seriousness, always with the aim of carrying out his duties, and that from then on it was good to let people know that such a danger was not the characteristic of a peculiar individual but came from a man who was like everyone else. And I realised that one also had to distinguish what a man does from what he is. And I also realised that being guilty for what one has done does not have any bearing on what one is.

'I'm afraid I also understood that the situation in which Duch found himself was not one that allowed him to backtrack. Not just from fear of dying, which he wouldn't have failed to do, but simply because under the gaze of others, in relation to the engagements one takes on when one goes underground – one is in a group, one is in a family, and it's certainly very difficult to get out of that. The trap closed over him. That is what continues to make me tremble today, Your Honour. I have finished my deposition.'

PRESIDING JUDGE:

'In order to continue, I would now like to ask the Magistrates if they wish to ask our witness questions. Examining Magistrate Lavergne.'

MAGISTRATE LAVERGNE:

'Thank you for your testimony. I am going to try to ask you a certain number of questions to clarify its import. First of all, concerning the facts of the camp itself. You indicated that, in your opinion, there were between forty and fifty inmates. Did you find out whether these inmates came from a particular category of the Cambodian population? Were they prisoners of war, people from the countryside, people from the towns? Was there a lot of change in this population – was there an influx in people, even if the term isn't very elegant, were there new arrivals?'

WITNESS:

'Yes, in fact, I think it was about fifty people. During the time I was there, that is, and I only stayed for three months. From what I could see, there were many more peasants, who lived in the regions under control of the Khmer Rouge. The influx . . . to use your term, Magistrate Lavergne, excuse me, so the . . . arrivals of new prisoners most of the time were prisoners who came alone, or accompanied, possibly, as I remember the man who came with his little daughter, or who arrived in twos or threes, and they probably came from the same regions. The problem was located, I think, on the border region between the territories controlled by the Khmer Rouge, from that military region in the southwest which formed a real bastion, and then the regions that were in contact with the regions said to be controlled by the pro-government people. Apparently M-13 was already – I'm not sure about this – but, it was oriented as a police centre linked to counter-espionage, in any case the majority of prisoners seemed to almost always represent people who had been found in a zone where they weren't known, where they couldn't give an explanation for their presence, and so many of the people who travelled a little between the two zones could have fallen under the definition of "spies". On the other hand, I witnessed the arrival of soldiers, when night was falling on the camp; they had bare feet, there were about twenty or thirty of them, and their arrival had put the camp into turmoil because no preparations had been made for their arrival. Their destination had been improvised or misdirected. They just spent that night at M-13 and I think the place hadn't been conceived to receive prisoners of war.'

MAGISTRATE LAVERGNE:

'You described to us the situation that had been reserved for you, I would like you to give a little more detail about the situation of your other . . . fellow inmates, to use the expression you yourself used. You had said that they were shackled, that their feet were in shackles. Can you tell us what the hygienic conditions were in which they lived? How could they satisfy their natural needs? Could they wash themselves? Did they have enough to eat?'

WITNESS:

'All the prisoners, except for a few rare exceptions, remained shackled to a common bar, on which bent pieces of metal, shaped like horseshoes, could slide, and these surrounded the ankle. Each of the three barracks, the floors of which were about eight centimetres above the ground, could hold about twenty prisoners, maybe thirty. One of them seemed reserved for the sick, but the other two were full. As to hygiene, they were not allowed to wash themselves, apart from when it rained as was often the case, to sprinkle themselves with rainwater without disturbing everyone with the help of containers used to urinate in. These were wide tubes cut from a kind of giant bamboo of the Cambodian forest, the kind used to harvest palm sugar, hanging at the ends of the barracks. To relieve the bowels, that was another problem. The prisoners talked with horror about the experience of going to the latrine. This was a hole, full of faecal matter, thinned out by mudslides, above which the prisoner had to squat, one foot on each of the slippery boards placed across a hole that was perhaps five feet wide. The fear of falling into it terrified everyone, all the more so since I think such a thing actually happened.'

MAGISTRATE LAVERGNE:
    'Food. What can you tell us about that?'

WITNESS:
    'Meals were distributed twice a day. They consisted of a plate of succulent rice cooked that morning by some of the prisoners, two if I remember correctly, who had the advantage of not being chained up all the time, and taken from the supply that the peasants from the neighbouring village, Thmar Kok, brought us. I repeat, this rice was succulent, in any case that's what I remember, and I don't know if it's hunger or really the quality of the rice that made me think that, but it was the only thing.

You could eat as much rice as you wanted, or in any case the plate was full, but there was nothing else.'

MAGISTRATE LAVERGNE:

'Was the diet the same for all the inmates, or do you think you received special treatment?'

WITNESS:

'I was going to add that, sir. I did benefit from special treatment, if I remember rightly, starting from the time Duch thought I wasn't guilty of the accusations made against me. And for me to remain in good health, I was allowed to share the guards' soup. Apart from my case, the prisoners' diet was the same for everyone. I should point out that the guards' diet was an extremely frugal meal.'

MAGISTRATE LAVERGNE:

'Considering the various categories of inmates. You spoke of inmates who were chained up, shackled, and you spoke of worker inmates, who didn't have any chains. Was that a daytime arrangement, was the system at night the same? Were they shackled at night? Were there a lot of those unchained inmates, or not?'

WITNESS:

'There weren't many of them, they were employed in the kitchens. From what I can remember of those details, I can't answer the specific questions you ask, namely if they were chained up at night if they weren't during the day. I would tend to think not, but I'm not sure. One of them ran away when I was there. And that put the guards into turmoil. Some of them chased him and came back declaring he had been caught and killed on site. I don't know if that's true. But that worker, whom I saw stacking up the rice every morning, and who often brought me my share himself, was very silent, and I think we all dreamed about his escape, picturing ourselves in his place. There were a lot of people who moved about in the camp, but I always understood that they were prisoners who had been there a long time, and who had in a way earned the right not to be chained up, because of their work, their submission to the conditions imposed on them.'

MAGISTRATE LAVERGNE:

'You spoke before about the guards, their childish behaviour, their very young age. Can you give us more details on the situation of these guards? Were they all children, were there adults, was there a hierarchy?'

WITNESS:

'I don't know if there was actually a hierarchy among the guards, I don't think so. On the other hand, they did have superiors, or adjutants if they can be called that, like Duch, who was the oldest one in the camp, and other younger leaders whom I saw appear without remembering them well, especially a young man who came several times and organised the discussion around the confessions, at night between the young guards; indoctrination meetings, in a way. On the other hand, there were a lot of squabbles between them. They were good peasant kids, they came from the surrounding villages, I'm certain about that for many of them since I was authorised, I remember, in preparing the farewell dinner that I mentioned at the start of my deposition, to accompany one of them to . . . it wasn't really a village but separate houses, in the middle of a clearing in the forest, anyway . . . to his mother's house, to order and pay for the thirteen chickens we needed, according to my estimate. So the guards were boys from the region. In a way, they benefited, if only in terms of food, and I also imagine, in the minds of their leaders, from this protection of the people won over to the revolution, who accepted that their own children would join the revolutionaries. That protected them in a way. Their behaviour among themselves was that of children who were having fun, who were cruel and perverse, and at the same time kind and nice. I had the same guards for three months, and from one day to the next their mood changed, their behaviour was unstable, and you couldn't expect the one who seemed accommodating on Monday to still be that way on Tuesday.'

MAGISTRATE LAVERGNE:

'Let's discuss the interrogations, then. You mentioned a gentle method. Is that a term you heard? Were those the words used when you were at M-13?'

WITNESS:

'No, Magistrate Lavergne. I think, when I used that word, I was using an anachronism. In fact, I knew, since I'd read about it, that in S-21 there was a gentle method and a harsh method. When I said that, I didn't mean to refer to any particular technique, I simply meant that I wasn't beaten, let's say tortured, to force me to confess. That's what I meant to say.'

MAGISTRATE LAVERGNE:

'You indicated that you were asked to write up a declaration of innocence. That is the word you used. So I would like to know if in fact they asked you to write such a declaration so described, or did they ask you to write confessions?'

WITNESS:

'Maybe it was a little like that, but I remember, unless I invented that term in the meantime, that I always recalled it as a 'declaration of innocence', that is, a text I had to write, in order to declare I was innocent of the accusations against me. That was normally the development, or the second part, of a curriculum vitae where I was supposed to describe my identity, to mention all the details about my father and mother, and also to explain the reasons, since I was a foreigner, that had made me come to Cambodia. I had to swear on oath, and I should say that to give more consistency and truth to what I was affirming, I wrote constantly, or at least each time: I swear on the head of my daughter that I was never . . . , etc. In a way, I had to say that I was innocent.'

MAGISTRATE LAVERGNE:

'You also spoke to us about what you were able to see, in a hut on the other shore of the river, and the deductions you made based on what you saw. Were you, however, a direct witness to any scene of violence? Did you hear shouts, did you hear things that, apart from what you saw, led you to think that violent practices were exercised?'

WITNESS:

'Never. I never heard shouts and I never witnessed any

violence, during the entire period of my incarceration in M-13. On the other hand, having been authorised to talk with my two co-workers, starting from the time when Duch agreed that both they and I be unchained, we had the opportunity to sit down together and talk a little. As I told you, sir, they were certain, without daring to tell me directly, that I would not be freed; in any case they feared it, and they told me that here the prisoners were beaten, that they were hit with sticks, on their ribs, and that since each prisoner wore a shirt – the black shirt with buttons – even if it was torn they kept wearing it, so that no one could see the traces of the blows they might receive. I don't think I'm mistaken in recalling this point, which was revealed to me by my two companions.'

MAGISTRATE LAVERGNE:

'Can you tell us a little also about the conversations you had with Duch about the relations between the Khmer Rouge and the Vietcong communists?'

WITNESS:

'Among the first things I think I said to Duch was this statement, this observation that everyone made, which was: but you yourselves, the Khmer Rouge, are in cahoots with the North Vietnamese. Do you imagine that once you're together and you win, that they'll leave? They'll give way to you? I think by saying that, by conveying my mistrust of the Vietnamese divisions that had entered Cambodia using as their sole recommendation the name of Sihanouk and a cigarette – they were entering the villages, I saw them come into Srah Srang, handing out a cigarette to the peasants they met on the way and uttering the only

Cambodian word they knew how to say, which was 'Sihanouk'. I'm just reporting a fact. By conveying this mistrust, I was agreeing with the party line, which apparently was already at that time in the process of distancing itself from this collaboration, if you can call it a collaboration, with the great neighbouring brother. I had also stressed that when the North Vietnamese divisions arrived in the region of Siemreap, and that the village where I lived 13 kilometres north of it, was itself on the other side of the Vietnamese lines that circled the city, I attempted to leave to go to the Angkor Conservation Centre where I worked, as I did every morning, without realising that the roads were cut off and that the North Vietnamese army was already in place. I was immediately arrested and led two hours later before a non-commissioned officer in his fifties who questioned me rapidly.

'That Vietnamese officer gave me a pass to go back to my village. Later, I never went anywhere without this pass on me. I have it here with me. It says in Vietnamese to let Comrade Bizot pass to go to his home, in terms that are vague enough to let it be useful. And when I found myself in charge of a job at the French School of Asian Studies (EFEO) in Phnom Penh, I continued to use this pass for the good reason that you risked meeting up with North Vietnamese troops more often than the Khmer Rouge, who were still not very present. All this to say that at the time of my arrest, I had thought that the presence of this pass on me would be perceived favourably. I found out later that on the contrary it had been held against me. As for Duch, insofar as he ever expressed himself on this point in front of me, I don't remember well, I think he himself was very aware of the risk that the Vietnamese forces represented on Cambodian territory.'

MAGISTRATE LAVERGNE:

'So you were freed, and you wrote a book called *The Gate* . . . in what year did you write that book?'

WITNESS:

'I wrote the book in 2000, sir.'

MAGISTRATE LAVERGNE:

'On page 6 [p. 26 of the French edition] of this book, you wrote: "A turn of bad luck made me one of them [speaking of the witnesses]. On October 10, 1971, while conducting research at a monastery in the region of Oudong, thirty kilometers north of Phnom Penh, I was arrested and then chained up in a Khmer Rouge detention camp. For three months, I saw the abomination spread its cloak over the countryside. As soon as I was released, the French Embassy asked me to translate a booklet on the 'Political Programme of the United National Front of Kampuchea' that I had brought from the bush. Its contents foreshadowed the horror: already there was mention of the evacuation of the towns and the establishment of a state-controlled collectivism based on a reduced population. But these warnings, duly relayed to Paris, had fallen on deaf ears, and France stubbornly maintained its support for the Khmer Rouge." So, I would like to know, about what you report in this document, do these documents correspond to what you described in your book or do you have another memory of them?'

WITNESS:

'It was during the dinner that was organised for my departure by the Khmer Rouge leaders of the region of Omleang that the senior official at this dinner – there were eight or nine people there, but he was the one who always monopolised the conversation to talk to me, laugh, make political commentaries on the future victory of the Khmer Rouge – told me after a while what he wanted, since the Khmer Rouge were already present in the city of Phnom Penh but that it was difficult for the revolutionaries to have access to the embassies. And he asked me if I would agree to take back documents to my country's embassy. I accepted these documents that were given to me in an envelope, which I immediately slipped into my shirt. I just insisted that they not be too bulky, for fear of being searched on my way.

'In fact, my liberation, which had been obtained after a hard internal fight amongst the Khmer Rouge, led also to my return to Phnom Penh, republican territory, where it was likely that I would arouse some suspicion, given the fact that till now the only prisoners released had been released by the Vietnamese. The Khmer Rouge took no prisoners. These documents contained two booklets printed in Khmer. I can't really remember the title or the contents that well. I translated this text myself, with a thief's precautions, because I was afraid of being caught in possession of this document, if my house was searched, which would have meant, at the very least, my expulsion from Cambodia. And that was the only thing I didn't want. I wanted to stay in Cambodia, with my family, and to keep doing the work I loved. That was my only concern.

'So I quickly translated this text, which was difficult to do, and I relayed the text to the French Embassy, along with photos they had entrusted me with also. There were about twenty photos, all from the period, which showed Khmer Rouge fighters, their weapons possibly, in a certain way, I've thought about it since, the photos also attested to the existence of certain people in the Khmer Rouge regime who were said to be suppressed by the party; especially Hou Youn and Hu Nim, but who seemed quite alive.

'When I decided to write my book, I realised that I had trouble recalling certain details from that time of my life, when the details didn't have to do with my feelings or emotions. I wrote the book not as a report, or as a testimonial, but on the basis of a feeling. And when it comes to a political text, how could I be in a position to speak of it or refer to it? I was lucky enough to find a trace of this document in the Quai d'Orsay archives, and since thirty years hadn't yet passed, I had to ask for special authorisation. Thus I was able to obtain a copy, not unfortunately of my translation, or of the original text that went with it, but of the summary that the chargé d'affaires, Mr Amiot, had made of it right away. So it's merely a summary of my translation that is in the archives. This text, very watered down, which I read, doesn't say much, and seemed to me to be greatly lacking in interest. At least the title is there, and I faithfully reproduced it in my book.'

MAGISTRATE LAVERGNE:

'So, I will point out that verifications have been made by the examining magistrates concerning these alleged documents, requests have been sent to Foreign Affairs, and two documents bearing the title "Political Programme of the United National Front of Kampuchea" have been found. They figure in the dossiers, listed as E27–1–3 and E27–1–4. I don't know if you had any particular occasion to read these documents, but I think it's easy to agree that they do not correspond to the description made of them in your book. In any case, I didn't see any mention of evacuation of cities, or of setting up a state-wide collectivism based on a reduced population.'

WITNESS:

'That's true, that is not in the summary.'

MAGISTRATE LAVERGNE:

'So, you think you were eventually able to reconstruct a memory and to include in it what you reported in your book, or is it something that existed in 1971?'

WITNESS:

'All possibilities should be taken into account, sir. That said, I remember that I had difficulty translating this text and in particular that there was a term that I translated as "nobs", because it was a neologism that I had trouble understanding and it seemed to me that "the rich" didn't quite measure up. I don't think I elaborated on this text beyond its contents, which I mostly remembered, but without any specific details. It is likely that the terms I use in the book are terms that were used later, both in the papers and in the often-repeated clichés, "local collectivism", "reduced population", etc., and that these exact terms, I used them concerning a text of which I remembered only the general tenor.'

MAGISTRATE LAVERGNE:

'Last question. You mentioned the analysis, the questioning, your analysis of human behaviour that Duch aroused in you. I am going to read a sentence from your book, *The Gate*, page. 279, where you wrote: "Time etches people from our past deep in our memories, and even if they have been an instrument of our unhappiness, they eventually arouse a sort of affection within us." I should point out that when you write this sentence you are speaking not of Duch, but of someone named Duong, who in fact was a person who had arrested you in 1971. Still, does this sentence also apply to Duch, for you?'

WITNESS:

'*The Gate* was written thirty years later, through remembering my fears, my emotions, my feelings at the time, which have never left me for thirty-eight years now. What I say about Duch and M-13, then, is what I saw with my own eyes, experienced and felt at the time and according to the traces left in me by these feelings. It's a literary process, which rests on a reconstruction, fed by reminiscences, which allows for my finding, through the images that remained with me, perhaps not the chronology, but a certain truth or exactitude of situations that occurred under my eyes in that camp. The statements that were made by Duch or by me, or by the guards, which I report, were written not on the basis of exact words that they uttered but on that of the content of the exchanges, and on what they meant.

'Now, you are referring to a precise point, the affection one can keep for certain things, even if they have been the instrument of our unhappiness. I should say that my meeting with Duch marked my fate and my entire thought, as well as everything I am today, for a simple and tragic reason. It's that I must henceforth come to terms as well as I can with a twofold given, both of whose aspects contradict each other terribly in me: on one hand a man who was the bearer, the armoured fist, of state-sponsored killing, and full of so many horrors committed that I can't imagine taking his place today; on the other hand a young man in whom I confess I am afraid of recognising myself, who has committed his life and his heart to the revolution, for an aim whose greatness supported the idea that crime was not only legitimate but praiseworthy, as it is in all wars.

'I don't know what to make of this contradiction, sir. My existence has led me to cross paths with both of these aspects of man at the same time, and I cannot rid myself of the thought that what was perpetrated by Duch could have been perpetrated by many other people. In wanting to think about this, it is not a question of minimising the gravity, the depth, the abomination of the crime that is his for a single instant. That is where things become particularly difficult for me, for I have felt that to take the measure of all the abomination, it would certainly not be by making Duch into a special monster that you would succeed in doing this. On the contrary it was by rehabilitating in him the humanity that is his as well as ours, by fully recognising it in him, and recognising that this humanity obviously was not an obstacle to the killings he carried out. Consequently, far from awakening in me any sort of "affection" [for the defendant], it is quite the contrary: this realisation of the characteristics and ambiguity that form our humanity is at the origin of my tragedy today, sir.'

MAGISTRATE LAVERGNE:

'Your Honour, if you will allow me, I would like to ask some questions of the defendant himself.'

PRESIDING JUDGE:

'Please do, you can ask your questions, the defendant is permitted to remain seated where he is to answer.'

MAGISTRATE LAVERGNE:

'So, my first question is the following. You remember that when I asked you questions about the hygienic conditions of the prisoners, you stated very firmly that the inmates were allowed to go and wash themselves in the river. You have just heard what the witness said, he said that he was the only one to have that privilege. So I would like to know what you have to say on this very precise point.'

DEFENDANT:

'Neither of us has betrayed the truth, sir. When Mr Bizot was with me, we were both near a small stream of deep water about thirty centimetres wide. So he is right to report that at that time the inmates were not allowed to wash themselves in that stream. As to what I myself said the day before yesterday, it was a question of another site, near a river.'

MAGISTRATE LAVERGNE:

'So, if I understand what you say, it's that at the time when Mr Bizot was detained, the other inmates were not allowed to clean themselves at the river.'

DEFENDANT:

'Yes.'

MAGISTRATE LAVERGNE:

'You also heard the witness say that lies were the oxygen breathed at M-13. And what's more that there was the presence of death, very strong, and he also reported what you told him about "torture", since that is the word that was used. So, I would like to know what you think about that, and then I will have one other question.'

DEFENDANT:

'Concerning torture, I have already explained this to the court. First of all I practised torture on someone named Keo Boun Hieng. So it is possible that it is this story I told Mr Bizot. About the little hut he saw, where there were chains and rings, I don't think he is wrong. On the other hand this building was not mine. I want to point out that before the creation of M-13, there was already at that spot a police station, which Ta Mok had destroyed, and that was headed by people from Hanoi. So it is possible, either that the building came from them, I don't know, or that it's the remains of a former building left on site. Concerning the tortures I don't dispute them. According to what was done, there were at least two ways to proceed, that I remember. That's all I wanted to say.'

MAGISTRATE LAVERGNE:

'What is this police station run by people from Hanoi?'

DEFENDANT:

'What I can reply from memory is that it was a police headquarters similar to M-13. But Ta Mok had it demolished before M-13 was created. When I was given leadership of M-

13, I also asked about it. Why did Ta Mok destroy this head-quarters of people from Hanoi? I asked this in order to be sure that what I was doing wouldn't suffer the same fate, but didn't receive a reply.'

MAGISTRATE LAVERGNE:

'I am going to read another extract from Mr Bizot's book, from a passage on page 112 [p. 184 of the French]. This is the conversation between you and François Bizot.

'François Bizot says this: "I thought I overheard something about prisoners in our camp being tied up and beaten . . . " Your reply: "'Most of the people who arrive here,' he explained after a short silence, 'have been caught in the act of spying. It's my responsibility to interrogate them, to find out who their contacts are, what type of information they're looking for, and who's paying them. Just one of these traitors could jeopardize our whole struggle. Do you think they're going to reveal what they know of their own free will?'" François Bizot asks: "'But who does the beating?' 'Ah!' he cut in", so you are giving your reply. "'I can't stand their duplicity! The only way is to terrorize them, isolate them, and starve them. It's very tough. I have to force myself. You cannot imagine how much their lying infuriates me! When I cross-examine them and they resort to every ruse to avoid talking, denying our senior officers potentially vital information, then I beat them! I beat them until I'm out of breath.'" Does what is reported in this book correspond to something that awakens memories in you, something that corresponds to a certain reality?'

DEFENDANT:

'I continue to believe that the story that Mr Bizot reports is exactly that of the interrogation I conducted on the spy named Keo Boun Hieng. At that time, as I have already told the court or a co-prosecutor – I'm not sure, I was suffering from malaria, I was having vertigo spells. As I was questioning him, two comrades from Hanoi intervened in order to hit him with full force, and he immediately confessed to being a spy. Seeing that, I got angry. I went over to him to kick him and the man begged me to stop. I raised my hand to hit him, but I was out of breath, tired to death. So I had him brought back to his place. It's that time that I felt out of breath, and that I was losing my balance. I felt very sick and extremely weak, because of my poor health. But it was also when the two comrades hit the prisoner in front of me that my emotion became very intense.'

MAGISTRATE LAVERGNE:

'Excuse me for interrupting you, but are we to understand from what you say that what Mr Bizot reports does not correspond to what you told him? Is it the truth or is it not the truth?'

DEFENDANT:

'I didn't read the passage written by Mr Bizot very carefully. But the story I remember is the one I have just told you. For now, in this moment when I am before you, I am not in a position to object to the statements made by Mr Bizot. I would like you to let us think it over together.'

MAGISTRATE LAVERGNE:

'So, just one clarification. You have this book in your possession. It was handed to you by your lawyers. Did you not read it?'

DEFENDANT:

'[Switches to French.] Of course I haven't [read it]. Only to page 122 [where] he wrote [about] the loss of Lay and Son.'

MAGISTRATE LAVERGNE:

'You remember the exact page, but you no longer remember what was written concerning torture?'

DEFENDANT:

'Yes . . . I think that what is related about torture all the violence represents the exact truth! And I can say this: when Mr Bizot was with me I did not hit him, I did not punish him, I did nothing to him. I saw that his greatest suffering came from [his responsibility to] Lay and Son.'

MAGISTRATE LAVERGNE:

'I have one final question. Much has been made about your desire to know the truth, and about your hatred of lying. I would like to know if you can confirm what is listed under D67 in the dossier. This is about one of your interrogations. And the co-examining magistrates asked you the following question.

'The question asked is the following: "This leads to asking you about the value you give the content of the confessions. Did you think they reflected the truth? Did your feelings on this evolve over the years?" You explain a certain number of things about S-21; maybe we'll go back to that later on. But you also say this, a little later: "Actually, at M-13, I already knew that the confessions did not reflect the truth. I was forced to work in the service of a criminal organisation my entire life and I assume my responsibility for that." Have you heard what I have just read, and have you understood it? Do you have any comments to make about it?'

Defendant:

'I heard clearly, and understood the statement you've just made. It's a question there of my analysis of confessions extracted under torture. And I acknowledge that it is a matter of crimes that cannot be denied.'

Magistrate Lavergne:

'My question is more precise. To quote you verbatim: "At M-13, I already knew that the confessions did not reflect the truth." So, do you confirm that you knew that the confessions were contrary to the truth?'

Defendant:

'I maintain that the confessions thus obtained did not reflect the truth. At the most, possibly just 20 per cent. And as to people whose names were given [in the course of these interrogations], at most 10 per cent.'

Magistrate Lavergne:

'Was there any kind of "political" truth, a truth that had to be in keeping with a proletarian line, I don't know how to qualify it, which caused you to cover up the fact that it wasn't reality?'

Defendant:

'Can you give me some time to think? I find that hard to answer. Can you rephrase your question, please, without changing it, but cutting it into smaller parts?'

MAGISTRATE LAVERGNE:

'You said that only 20 per cent of confessions were in keeping with the truth. My question is the following, were they in keeping with a truth that was not reality, but that was the truth desired by the party, by the proletarian line, by the ideology?'

DEFENDANT:

'The 20 per cent I refer to as not reflecting the truth can be explained this way. Among the many people who were arrested and who had to be interrogated, some were revolutionaries accused of being informers. Let me take the example of the confession of Khoy Thuon. I did not personally read his confessions, but the upper echelons who learned about them told me that they were true. Still, as far as I was concerned, that posed a problem. I didn't know what to believe between his activities as a traitor and his revolutionary activities, as soon as he acknowledged he was under the orders of the CIA. So, the reason I say that these confessions were not truthful, comes from this contradiction.'

MAGISTRATE LAVERGNE:

'One final question. You also heard what was said about delation. Do you know what "delation" means . . . You didn't hear the question?'

DEFENDANT:

'Yes, I heard the question but I don't understand the word "delation".'

MAGISTRATE LAVERGNE:

'Informing is the act of denouncing. Was denunciation part of the principles that had to be implemented in order to become a good revolutionary? Was it, you heard what was said before, was it highly regarded, for instance, to denounce one's own parents?'

DEFENDANT:

'That is a question that has to do with theory. I heard talk of it, already when I was in the main prison. They said a certain Vietnamese officer had had his own father arrested. When his father was presented to him, he said: "I respectfully greet my father, but I am going to have the enemy executed." Personally, I never appreciated it when my subordinates denounced their parents. I never encouraged that.'

PRESIDING JUDGE:

'Now, the Court would like to give the stand to the co-prosecutors.

FOREIGN CO-PROSECUTOR:

'[. . .] Thank you, Your Honour. Mr Bizot, a few questions. Perhaps it's a question of translation, but yesterday you told us, very eloquently, about the last meal before your liberation and, especially, the conversation you had with the defendant, in which he confessed to you to having himself beaten the prisoners to make them confess. However, you seemed, and once again I beg your indulgence if the translation wasn't faithful, but you seemed to say Duch also told you this work made him vomit. I think I have looked at your book attentively

– excuse me; reread your book – reread the transcript of your questioning by the examining magistrate, and I did not see anywhere at any time, even less during that meal, the defendant, during those three months, express to you any remorse or any anxiety about, and once again you'll excuse me, this work. So, could you clarify if in fact you maintain today or remember today this apparent remorse that he expressed to you during that supper or dinner, or if it might perhaps be a question of a hope you may have had or a memory, a memory you have kept?'

WITNESS:

'Yes, Mr Prosecutor, I myself am troubled about one point in particular. It is one thing to testify objectively about what happened in front of my eyes. But quite another to relate through writing what I experienced. Although the degree of exactitude of the events and facts that occurred and that I relate in my book does not go beyond my memories, I did not see everything – far from it. And someone else would have said things differently, and seen things that I did not see. All the more so since I did not solicit, how can I say it, my conscious memory, in a certain way, to report thirty years after the fact on the effects produced on me by an ordeal that I was not supposed to emerge from alive. So in this book, I expressed a feeling. To give testimony now on what happened during three months, thirty-eight years afterwards, is another affair, and I ask on my part for infinitely more verbal precautions. I should say, to answer your question, that I did not hear Duch express remorse. I think I recall . . . I was going to say the extreme awkwardness, or how should I say, the great discomfort, of

Duch when he told me he sometimes hit prisoners. He should not have told me; I would not have imagined it. But since he told me, I remember it. The terms he used to say it, I can't confirm them. I simply remember that it was in a spirit of spontaneity, of sincerity, of the work he had to do and that he thought it was a work that he was forced to do, and he had to force himself to it. Force himself. That he was – how should I say it – doing his duty. If I said yesterday that it made him vomit, I think that . . ., no longer remembering what I said yesterday, that might not be the word he used.'

FOREIGN CO-PROSECUTOR:

'You agree with me, that having a duty does not necessarily imply forcing oneself to carry out that duty. Correct me again if I am mistaken, but you are telling us that at no time during your detention did the defendant express remorse to you, and that during that conversation you relate in another part of your book and in the official record of your questioning – and, let us understand each other, it is quite clear that thirty years later, in the circumstances that you experienced, we all understand that your testimony reflects these circumstances. But still, this obligation to do this kind of work, you do not relate it in these documents, and you tell us about it this morning. Would it be correct to say that it's rather an impression you had and not something that Duch said himself?'

WITNESS:

'He told me . . . that it was work that fell to him to do. And that . . . I'm afraid of not remembering what I wrote. You see, in some way, writing it washed my memory clean, emptied it out. I'm afraid I can't actually remember the memories that I had before writing that book. And I'm afraid of repeating to you what I wrote. Still, I think I remember that Duch said that he did this work without any pleasure, like an obligation, because the prisoners wouldn't tell the truth on their own.'

FOREIGN CO-PROSECUTOR:

'And, to be quite clear, this conversation took place when you were with other officials, including a leader, or were you on the contrary alone with Duch?'

WITNESS:

'No, it was the night before my liberation. I wasn't set free on the 24th but the 25th of December, and this setback that caused me to be freed a day later, created a sort of wait in the night. It was when I went over to Duch, who was sitting near the fire, or the other way round. There was no one else, except a young guard who came after a while and whom Duch asked to sing a revolutionary song.'

FOREIGN CO-PROSECUTOR:

'You testified to the examining magistrate, as well as yesterday, that you were not a victim of physical torture. But what about psychological torture? More precisely, you relate two incidents in your book. The first, in which the defendant made you think you were finally found out, found guilty, and that you would have to bear the consequences. This incident obviously created a reaction in you, and before this reaction Duch announced to you: "No, no, that's a joke! Ha! Ha!" Could you confirm whether in fact this incident occurred as I describe it, or if not, can you describe it yourself if I left out some details, and confirm that in fact this incident did occur?'

WITNESS:

'I can confirm it completely. The defendant is here to remember it. Although it is hard to remember certain words used at the time, either by him, or by me, on the other hand, this interlude, when he came back from one of his weekly excursions, is extremely clear in my memory. So I confirm that in fact there was joking about . . . how should I say it, about the finality of my detention. That is, he told me that, in a certain way, I had been found out and unmasked. I think that's the first and only time Duch spoke to me in French. My reaction was all the keener since I knew the night before that he would spend the day talking with leaders, his superiors, and that my case would be brought up again. And since I had already been there three months, it couldn't last much longer. When he pretended in front of me that I had been unmasked and that the accusations brought against me implicitly were correct, my knees gave way and I collapsed. Then he lifted me up and told me it was a joke.'

FOREIGN CO-PROSECUTOR:

'And could you tell us about the other incident of this kind, when the defendant used your relationship with your colleague and friend Son, also to make you believe in consequences, and later on telling you that it was also a joke?'

WITNESS:

'Mr Prosecutor, are you referring to what happened when my two companions had been untied and when I myself was free to move about the camp? That might also have happened when Duch ordered a young guard to unchain Lay and Son. Are you referring to the remark he made to Son? I should have reread my book before coming, since I no longer remember what I wrote. There was a scene when Duch, in a way, joked when he was talking to Son. Duch had understood that I was very attached to Lay. I had known Lay for over five years. We were together all the time, we worked together. Son had been employed by the Angkor Conservation for just six months, I think. He was a young married man, and I didn't have a lot to do with him, I didn't know him as well. So, when we were all three together, it was with Lay that there was direct communication, especially since he was more experienced at his work than Son. Duch said to Son: "Bizot is going to leave, but one of you has to stay. Since there's a choice, Bizot thought it was Lay who should leave with him." So, silence on Son's part. Then Duch said to him: "You believe me, you believe that's possible?" And, to my great dismay, Son replied: "Yes, I think it's possible." After which, I think Duch added, "Ah! Finally someone believes me." But he laughed, and Son was detached at the same time as Lay.'

FOREIGN CO-PROSECUTOR:
    'Thank you. No more questions.'

PRESIDING JUDGE:
    'I would like to continue by giving the plaintiffs a chance to ask the witness their questions. I would first like to invite the lawyers of plaintiffs from Group No. 1.'

FOREIGN CO-LAWYER FROM GROUP NO. 1:

'Hello, Mr Bizot. My name is Alain Verner, and I represent thirty-eight plaintiffs in this trial. I just have a few questions for you. The first question: you mentioned yesterday your special status at M-13. To use your words, you spoke of special treatment, especially concerning food at a certain time, and then also in relation to the fact that you were not beaten. It was clear in what you said yesterday and in your book that it was the defendant who granted you this preferential treatment. Do you know, Mr Bizot, if the defendant obtained preliminary authorisation from his superiors before granting you this preferential treatment?'

WITNESS:

'I can't know. I can't even say if I think so or not. I don't know at all, I can't answer your question.'

FOREIGN CO-LAWYER FROM GROUP NO. 1:

'Yesterday you mentioned the fact that the defendant spoke little and you said that he was very committed to his responsibility as camp leader. Mr Bizot, what did you see or what were you told that made you think this?'

WITNESS:

'That emerged from the visible personality of the defendant, already at the time and then from the reputation he had among the guards. The young guards had a lot of respect for the defendant on the basis of the many hours of work that he spent on the files; on the files, or in any case, he worked a lot. And that gave him a reputation as a serious, responsible person who inspired a certain respect among the guards. Later, I noticed that what I said or wrote in my statements was always compared with what I had said a week or two before, and this analysis of my assertions was done with care. Then, in the last two days, from the time when they took off my chains and I could speak with Lay and Son, and even exchange a few words with the prisoners, Duch enjoyed with everyone the reputation of being someone very committed to his various tasks.'

FOREIGN CO-LAWYER FROM GROUP NO. 1:

'I just have two more questions, Your Honour. The first one concerns the interrogations, Mr Bizot. You said yester-day: "I couldn't supply any proof of my non-guilt," and you explained that, at a certain time, you told yourself that you couldn't prove your innocence. And then, responding to Mr Petit, the Co-Prosecutor, you spoke of that example of a mock-execution. I just have one question about that, Mr Bizot. Do you think that a Cambodian, someone perhaps without your education, without your erudition as a Member of the French School of the Far East, that a Cambodian questioned by the defendant could supply proof of his non-guilt, as you yourself succeeded in doing?'

WITNESS:

'I don't think so. I'm not saying that I know that's not right, but that I don't think so. On the contrary, I think that, having arrived in the prison camp, there were no outcomes apart from guilt. I also have the feeling that all attempts to say that the accusations made against one were unjust, unfounded, only painfully delayed the moment of death. That's what I think. On the other hand, I do not have the impression of having succeeded in convincing the defendant of my non-culpability, myself. I think that was an idea he formed himself, on the basis of what I said during the interrogations and the crosschecks he made with Lay and Son on the reality of my activities. In a way, I benefited – I feel only suffering because of this – but the presence of Lay and Son in this camp was a fundamental factor in my liberation. Whatever I said on one side could only be confirmed by their memories on the other.'

FOREIGN CO-LAWYER FROM GROUP NO. 1:

'One last thing, Mr Bizot. During the many interviews you gave to the press, over the past few months and years, there is a recurrent term which is the fact that behind the mask of the monster you have to see the man, you have to manage to see the human being. And you yourself apparently succeeded in doing this, in relation to the defendant, and to see the man. Of course this procedure belongs to you, and for the plaintiffs, we respect it. I just have one question about it. You were not merely the victim of the defendant. You were detained by an organisation, the Khmer Rouge, and of course you know what it later went on to do to this country, which is a country you love. Are you still willing to see the man behind the torturer, in relation to the Khmer Rouge leaders still alive and awaiting trial, with whom you had no direct interaction – I'm thinking especially of Nuon Chea? Can you also see the man in him?'

WITNESS:

' . . . Yes, sir.'

FOREIGN CO-LAWYER FROM GROUP NO. 1:
'I have no other questions, Mr Pre . . . '

WITNESS:
'I haven't finished.'

FOREIGN CO-LAWYER FROM GROUP NO. 1:
'Excuse me.'

WITNESS:
'What I mean by that is that to take the measure of the abomination of the torturer and his actions, that it's especially about, you just cited the name of Nuon Chea. Or of the defendant. I say that we need to rehabilitate the humanity that inhabits him. If we make him into a special monster, in whom we are unable to recognise ourselves, as a human being, not as what he did but as a human being, the horror of his actions seems to escape us to a certain extent. So if we consider that he is a man with the same capacities as ourselves, we are frightened, beyond that kind of segregation that would have to be made between those who are capable of killing and us, who are not capable of it. Unfortunately I'm afraid that we have a more terrifying understanding of the torturer when we take account of his human side.

'Also, trying to understand is not wanting to forgive. It seems to me that there is no forgiveness possible. In the name of whom can we forgive? In the name of those who have died? I do not think so. And the horror of what was done in Cambodia, which is not exclusive unfortunately to that poor country, is a bottomless horror, and the cries of the victims should be heard without ever thinking they could be excessive. The harshest words that one can use against the defendant are words that can never be harsh enough. It is not a question of wanting to forgive what was done. My approach (which doesn't have to be that of the victims) is trying to understand the universal tragedy that was played out here, in the forests of Cambodia; as in other countries, or at other times in our history. Even the most recent history.'

PRESIDING JUDGE:

'Now, I would like to give the floor to the lawyers from the plaintiffs in Group No. 2. You may proceed.'

FOREIGN CO-LAWYER FOR GROUP NO. 2:

'Thank you, Your Honour. My name is Silke Studzinsky and I am a co-lawyer for the plaintiffs from Group 2.

'Mr Bizot, I would like to go back over your relationship to the defendant, in the course of your three-month stay, which you report in the English translation of your book, as being characterised by a certain familiarity. Could you tell us how often and on what sort of subjects, if you remember, you were able to communicate and maintain a sort of intellectual exchange, as I understood it yesterday, with the defendant.'

WITNESS:

'I saw the camp leader, Duch, almost every day. I myself was unable to contain my tears, my suffering, and the feeling of incomprehension, injustice, that I was experiencing. This was conveyed, most of the time, through anger. An anger that was quite pointless, which I exercised finally only against myself, but during the interrogations, faced with the questions Duch asked me, which gave me the strength to express the unbearable injustice I was the victim of as well as experiencing the relief of asking questions myself in return to my interrogator. I should say that he got caught up in this too, that he spoke to me about his family, maybe so that – and I'm adding this – I would speak more about my own. He spoke to me about his work, at the time when he was teaching maths in Kompong Thom, maybe also so that I would speak more about my work. All that went towards creating a certain regularity in the daily relations we had, when we resumed discussions from the day before; he would eventually return to the points of information I had provided, but presuming that I'd skipped things – in short, he was doing his work as an interrogator. All that created in the end a sort of daily ritual, a habit.

'I think that if following this ordeal of imprisonment I received a shock that I cannot forget, which was seeing the man behind the torturer, Duch, for his part, in a way got from me what no torturer should do: he himself was led to see the man behind the spy, behind the prisoner. And I am convinced that the leader of M-13 was led to regard my file with an attention that he could not bring to the others, because my interrogation, which lasted a long time, created a sort of link of humanity between us. In so doing, sending me to my death became a much more difficult operation than having dehumanised people killed, or people he didn't seek to humanise. I don't know, sir, if I have answered your question.'

FOREIGN CO-LAWYER FOR GROUP NO. 2:
    'Yes, thank you. I will go back over part of my question. Would it be true to say that this return questioning, how should

I say, the questions you asked him in replying to his, took the form of a discussion, rather than an interview, and not an interrogation? More like an exchange?'

WITNESS:

'I would not say that. These exchanges, these discussions, revolved around a very clear, precise objective: catching me in the wrong. Leading me to contradict myself. I don't know if the coherence of all my answers was satisfying, but in any case a certain number of elements emerged from it for him, allowing him to think that I was not a CIA agent. That is what he stressed to his superiors. I do not think, except maybe the final day once I was freed from my chains, that there was ever any sort of simple, free friendship between us. The context we found ourselves in was too infernal. You can't speak of normal relations between a jailer and a prisoner, even less in a camp like that one.'

FOREIGN CO-LAWYER FOR GROUP NO. 2:

'Thank you, Mr Bizot.'

PRESIDING JUDGE:

'I invite the lawyers for the plaintiffs from Group No. 3 to ask their questions. You have the floor.'

FOREIGN CO-LAWYER FOR GROUP NO. 3:

'Thank you, Your Honour. Mr Bizot, my name is Philippe Cannone, and I am in charge of the defence of the interests of Group 3 of the plaintiffs [. . .] I would like to know, Mr Bizot, if you found out, during the time of your detention, the number of executions carried out.'

WITNESS:

'I believe I guessed at that in my book; these things are not clear now in my memory. Executions were hard to guess, since I saw people come in and go out. I always had the impression that the ones that went out did so to be executed. But to reconstruct the number, like that, would, I think, be too much guesswork. There were also about fifteen people who died of malaria when I was there. Um . . . unfortunately I cannot be more precise on the number of executions that took place in M-13 during that period. I will add, though, that I think that all the prisoners I saw come in, and who were still alive when I left, must have died.'

FOREIGN CO-LAWYER FOR GROUP NO. 3:

'I'll return, Mr Bizot, to your own interrogations. Did it ever come about that falsified documents were presented to you about your alleged culpability, in order to confuse you?'

WITNESS:

'No, nothing like that ever happened.'

FOREIGN CO-LAWYER FOR GROUP NO. 3:

'I'll put aside the facts, Mr Bizot, since many questions have been asked of you. It seems to me that the lofty view you assumed earlier, the distance you willingly took, authorises me to question you about your feelings. Do you permit me to proceed this way with you?'

[WITNESS AGREES.]

'Good. So, my final question is twofold. During the preliminary investigation and detention of Duch, you asked to meet him. We understood – and I concur with my colleague Verner on the respect he testifies to in relation to this procedure – we understood your wish to try to understand the complexity of the human soul. Two half-questions, then. Today, does remorse or regret, which were not manifest back then at any time, as you said, come to Duch's mind? Second question. So you can answer both at once. When you left your comrades, they said to you: "French comrade, don't forget us!" If Lay and Son were here today, what would they expect from this confrontation, what would they expect from this trial, and please understand me, Mr Bizot, beyond those two companions, what can all these plaintiffs expect today?'

WITNESS:

'I cannot answer for Lay and Son. As for me, I do not authorise myself to assume the status of victim. If I try nonetheless to put myself in the place of those who have died under torture or afterwards, as you ask me to, I think that the only arrangement that could pacify me and lighten the inextinguishable the unstoppable execration that eats at me, the hatred . . . would be to feel I had got even. To find my compensation in the suffering inflicted on the torturer. I wonder, though, whether things could ever be so, and even whether such an equation has any meaning, considering the atrocity of the Khmer Rouge crimes. That being the case, since you address me in the name of my former co-prisoners, I do not think I betray them if I say that such a forgiveness on their part would have taken place only if Duch's losses seemed of a nature to annul their own. More simply, when the suffering imposed on the man who tortured my father, made my children die, became equal to the suffering endured by them.'

PRESIDING JUDGE:

'I now give the floor to the lawyers for the defence, so they can ask their questions of the witness, Mr François Bizot. You may proceed.'

MR ROUX:

'Thank you, Your Honour. Hello, Mr Bizot. Just a few questions, since many things have already been said. But perhaps one precise question concerning this assistant of Duch's. We have asked him the question. If I give you the name of Ho Kim Heng, alias Soum, could it be that person?'

WITNESS:

'Ho Kim Heng doesn't ring any bells. On the other hand, I have the impression that Soum could in fact correspond to the name I might remember.'

MR ROUX:

'Then I am going to ask you a few questions, or more precisely, ask you for your comments on previous statements you have made, especially to the examining magistrates [. . .] At the end of your deposition, you added: "You ask me if in conclusion I have a general observation to make. I will simply say that the Khmer Rouge regime was a regime of terror, and that it was probably very difficult for those who exercised a function in this regime to backtrack." A comment, Mr Bizot?'

WITNESS:

'I have nothing to add to what I said during that interview. I think in fact it's something that doesn't need to be proved or demonstrated that the Khmer Rouge regime was indeed a regime of terror, and I never once saw, where I was concerned, unless it's about my own liberation, that important decisions, of that kind for instance, were made on Duch's level. He had to refer to the higher echelon.'

MR ROUX:

'Thank you. So, continuing on the question of terror, you spoke more particularly of Duch himself in your book [...] You write: "And so he, like everyone from his fellow leaders to the humblest conscripts, was ruled by fear." In the pages that were read to you yesterday by Magistrate Lavergne, page. 112 [p. 185 of the French; translation slightly modified], I would like to mention one more passage. You write: "There was still generosity in him; perhaps the presence of a constant suffering, as visible in his posture as in his face, is what connected me to him." You speak of constant suffering, and you speak of it again to the examining magistrates, on page 5 of listing D40, you say: "I want to stress that if the guards were afraid of Duch, and the prisoners were terrified of Duch, he himself was also a victim of fear; in particular, I think his disagreement with Ta Mok about me pursued Duch for years." Duch, you told the examining magistrates, was afraid of Ta Mok. I would like your comments about this fear, this suffering, of which you apparently were a witness.'

WITNESS:

'I cannot attempt to remember the images that were still

present in my mind when I think of M-13, without remembering that frightening atmosphere that reigned, of fear and death. Or without remembering how embodied this atmosphere was in the camp's director, in the defendant, at the time. It reigned over everyone, and I do not think it is possible to imagine that it could be otherwise. When Duch went to his meetings and then came back, his face, his expression, showed a depletion that I could only connect to the various subjects he must have discussed when he spoke with his superiors. It was clear that every time it was a matter of deciding on the time for an already planned execution. At not a single instant in the existence of the camp leader, or of his assistants, were there exchanges whose content had to do with light subjects. This constant presence of an action that revolved completely around the suppression of life, around torture, could not have any other effect than those that we all felt physically.'

Mr Roux:

[. . .] 'Mr Bizot, when you answered particularly pertinent questions of certain lawyers for the plaintiffs, and I am thinking especially of that last question from my colleague Mr Cannone, you used words of great humanity about the victims. You also used words of great humanity during the entire discussion, about Duch. I would like to thank you in the name of the defence, Mr Bizot, for the major contribution you have made here to the work of justice.

'Thank you, Your Honour.'

Presiding Judge:

'Thank you, Mr François Bizot, for the testimony you have

just given the Court. The Court has no more questions. You
are free henceforth to sit in the public gallery or, if you prefer,
to go home. I now invite the Bailiff to escort you out of the
court.'

Acknowledgements

I have been collecting material for a hypothetical work for a long time (you never write the book that you want), which I was sure would somehow be dedicated to the people, books and things that I'd come across along the way and that had bestowed their gifts on me.

Nothing would have begun, and nothing would have been completed, without the friendship of Antoine Audouard, who accompanied me through the endless fluctuations, the setbacks, and the adventures of this book.

Susanna Lea's generosity and determination enabled it to be published internationally.

I was able to write this book in peace – albeit through hazardous thought processes that it took me years to disentangle – at Susanna and Antoine's home, in part in Chiang Mai, and in part in the Yonne, at Brigitte and Bubu's home where I removed myself to the greenhouse, under the 'onyx eyes' of a gentle Géline chicken who would come every morning to alight on my knees, reminding me of my M-13 friends.

This book would not have been the same either without the

eternal presence and force of my three children, Hélène, Charles and Laura, or the daily attention of each of my faithful boxers ('Avi').

I would like to express my gratitude to Teresa Cremisi for her loyalty and availability.

I am particularly indebted to Jean-Christophe Attias, Robert Baeli, Thierry Cruvellier, Marcel Lemonde, François Roux and Tzvetan Todorov.

In many respects the revision of the English translation has given me an opportunity to revisit and question the French text. This has been made possible by Antoine's personal commitment to helping its original music and meaning mutate into another language. I am also very grateful to Beth Humphries, who edited the manuscript with subtlety and insight. Last but not least, the enduring support and understanding of Judith Kendra have been invaluable.

Chronology of Events

1954   Cambodian independence declared. Full national sovereignty transferred to the king, Norodom Sihanouk. In Vietnam, the French are defeated at Dien Bien Phu; following the Geneva Agreements, the country is divided into two. The end of French Indochina, a colonial entity comprising Vietnam, Cambodia and Laos.

1960   Bizot's military service in Algeria.

1963   Death of Bizot's father.

1965   Bizot's departure for Cambodia.

1965–6   The United States sends in ground troops to protect South Vietnam from Communist invasion. The Khmer Communist movement, founded in 1951, sends a delegation to Peking and becomes known as the Kampuchea Communist Party (KCP).

1968–9   American troops in South Vietnam number 550,000. US air raids launched on Vietcong hideouts in Cambodia.

1969   *Coup d'état* on 18 March, in Phnom Penh. General Lon Nol, who supports US intervention, seizes power and proclaims the Khmer Republic. From Peking, Sihanouk calls for resistance and announces the formation of the Government of the Royal National Union of Kampuchea (GRNUK). American and South Vietnamese troops infiltrate Cambodia.

1970   The Vietcong invade Cambodia and occupy the site of Angkor.

1971   Bizot's arrest and detention in a Khmer Rouge extermination camp run by Duch (M-13). Duch intercedes with the hierarchy to have him released (10 October–25 December).

1973   Signing of the Paris Agreements and withdrawal of American troops. The KCP forces young peasants to enlist in the Revolutionary Army of Liberation.

1974   Start of the Khmer Rouge offensive against Phnom Penh (December).

1975   France recognises GRNUK (12 April). On 17 April, the capital falls. Evacuation of the towns. Bizot expelled to Thailand, together with all the foreigners who had found refuge inside the walls of the French embassy. Beginning of the 'purification' of all strata of the population. Opening of the Tuol Sleng torture camp at Phnom Penh (S-21), headed by Duch.

1976   Sihanouk resigns as head of state. Proclamation of Democratic Kampuchea, under the presidency of Khieu Samphan; Pol Pot is prime minister. Attempted putsch at Phnom Penh. Disbanding of the 'Pro-Vietnamese network'.

1977   Kampuchea's economy supported entirely by China. Diplomatic relations between Kampuchea and Vietnam broken off.

1978   Following a series of Khmer incursions into Vietnamese territory, Vietnamese divisions occupy the provinces to the east of the Mekong River.

1979–80   Major Vietnamese offensive; Phnom Penh captured on 7 January 1979. Government formed under Vietnamese military protection. Proclamation of the People's Republic of Kampuchea. Famine causes Khmer Rouge fighting units to disband, and their headquarters withdraw to Thailand. Duch flees and retreats with the rest of the armed forces to bases in the forest and along the frontier with Thailand.

1988   Bizot's return to Cambodia. He discovers the horrors of S-21 and recognises Duch in a photo of the prison's former director.

1989   Vietnamese troops capture several Khmer Rouge positions on the frontier with Thailand. Formal withdrawal of Vietnamese expeditionary force.

1991   International peace agreement signed in Paris.

1993   Numerous defections among Khmer Rouge ranks after elections organised by the United Nations.

1998   Death of Pol Pot. Collapse of the Khmer Rouge movement.

1999   Duch's arrest in Samlaut, near the Thai border. Bizot starts writing his account of his incarceration in *The Gate* (published in Great Britain in 2003).

2001   Establishment of the Extraordinary Chambers of the Courts of Cambodia (ECCC) to try crimes committed under the Democratic Kampuchea between 1975 and 1979.

2003   Bizot receives authorisation to visit Duch, in the Phnom Penh military prison. Shooting of a documentary surrounding his meeting with the torturer.

2008   Bizot's second meeting with Duch in the new ECCC prison.

2009   Beginning of Duch's public trial (February 17th). Bizot testifies before the court (8 and 9 April).

2010   Duch is sentenced to 35 years of imprisonment (26 July). He appeals the judgment.

2011   Beginning of the trial of the main Khmer Rouge leaders (June).

Notes

I. 1963 – SARAH

1 Friedrich Hölderlin, 'The Lines of Life' (quoted in Ernst Jünger, *The Paris Diaries*, 23 February, 1942, New York: Farrar Straus & Giroux, 1992).

2 The S-21 special jail was set by the Khmer Rouge in the former premises of the Tuol Sleng lycée in Phnom Penh. There, between 1975 and 1979, several tens of thousands were detained, tortured and sent to be executed in the 'Killing Fields' of Choeung Ek. Only seven prisoners survived.

3 Nathaniel Hawthorne, *The Scarlett Letter*.

4 Primo Levi, *The Drowned and the Saved*, New York: Vintage, 1989.

5 Nic Dunlop and Nate Thayer, 'Duch Confesses', *Far Eastern Economic Review*, 6 May, 1999; vol 170, no. 3. See also: Nic Dunlop, *The Lost Torturer – A Journey into the Heart of the Killing Fields*, New York: Walker, 2005.

6 *France-Soir*, 1945, in Joseph Kessel, *Jugements derniers* : les procès de Nuremberg, Paris: Tallandier, 2007.

7 Kessel, *Jugements derniers*.

8 Rudolf Hoess, *Le Commandant d'Auschwitz parle*, Paris: La Découverte Poche, 2005. (Rudolf Hoess, *The Commandant*, New York: Overlook Press, 2011. Rudolf Hoess, *Commandant of Auschwitz: The Autobiography of Rudolf Hoess*, London: Weidenfeld & Nicolson, 2000.)

9 *Ibidem*, p. 222.

10 Molière, *The Misanthrope*, trans. John Wood and David Coward, New York: Penguin, 2000, Act III, p. 121.

II. 1971 – THE REVOLUTIONARY

1 As recounted in Document 2, p. 152.

2 The issue of false confessions obtained under torture gives birth to total and widespread perplexity. 'This determination to break down the suspect mentally in order to finally prove nothing is completely insane' (Francis Deron, *Le procès des Khmers rouges, Trente ans d'enquête sur le génocide cambodgien*, Paris: Gallimard, 2009, p. 51). It raises a question that would come up repeatedly during Duch's trial. That said, it's worth wondering how pertinent the questions are in the case of interrogations whose goal was clearly never to uncover the 'truth' as we understand it, in accordance with common sense and reason. It is possible that we are adding a false dilemma to the simple horror (with Duch himself trying, in vain, to answer satisfactorily the judges: 20%, 50%, etc.), and that it is wrong to come back to it repeatedly, while the Khmer Rouge had implicitly dismissed it (cf. the witness's embarrassment when faced with Judge Lavergne's questions about the 'party's desired truth'– see Document 2, pp. 181–183).

3 Angkar, the 'Organisation,' stood for the most radical section of

the CPK (Communist Party of Kampuchea), which would take power in 1975. Under this anonymous appellation decisions were made and carried out at all levels and in all sectors in order to maintain secrecy and protect the Party's organisation. The rather vague name gave a particular force to the ruling party, creating and maintaining a feeling of uncertainty and fear. Every aspect of daily life fell under the authority of Angkar.

4 Quoted in David Chandler, *Voices from S-21: Terror and History in Pol Pot's Secret Prison*, London: University of California Press, 2000, p. 91.

5 Cf. Document 1, pp. 137–141. For a full account of my arrest, detention and release, see François Bizot, *The Gate*, London: Vintage, 2004.

6 Cf. Document 2, pp. 179–181.

7 'Permanence of man': chapter title of a book by Olga Wormser and Henri Michel, *Tragédie de la déportation* (Paris: Hachette, 1954), used here in contrast to the 'permanence of man' that the deportees often asserted just before dying.

8 Ho Kim Heng, alias Soum. This name, which I had forgotten, Duch reminded me of during my testimony before the court (cf. Document 1, p. 142. Document 2, p. 199).

9 To borrow the title from Joseph Conrad's famous story.

10 Christopher Columbus.

11 Cf. Emmanuel Levinas, *Ethics and Infinity: Conversations with Philippe Nemo*, trans. Richard A. Cohen, Pennsylvania: Duquesne University Press, 1985, 'Responsibility for the Other'.

12 Hannah Arendt, *Penser l'événement*, « Après le nazisme », Berlin: Habib, 1989.

III. 1988 – THE TORTURER

1 See Chronology of Events, p. 205.

2 See *The Gate*, pp. 143–266.

3 Monastic 'discipline', the 'rules' (Pali *vinaya*). No monk can ordain others without having ten years of service

4 Jacques Loiseleur was caught along the national road 5 after a clash between governmental and rebel forces. He was transporting fish from Kompong Chnnang to a local humanitarian organisation based in Phnom Penh that was battling hunger. In his Battambang interviews, Duch remembers the truck driver who was greatly influenced by Catholicism and with whom he spent one Christmas Day. Loiseleur was executed in 1973. In relation to this, Duch explained that, after 1975, Nuon Chea's instruction was to burn the bodies of foreigners using tyres, so as not to leave any trace. (Cf. also Document 1, p. 144).

5 Anatole France, *Thaïs*, Paris: Actes Sud, 1992.

IV. 1999 – THE INMATE

1 Nate Thayer. The Americian journalist (from the *Far Eastern Economic Review*) was in Battambang with Duch, from whom he obtained the first declarations.

2 The main execution site and mass grave of the Tuol Sleng prison, 15 km southwest of Phnom Penh. The site had been known for the footprint of Buddha on view in the local monastery, Choeug Ek Wat (The stupa of the 'Only Foot') which I visited on many occasions (see 'La Figuration des pieds du Bouddha au Cambodge', *Études asiatiques*, Berne 1971).

3 'Apprendre à avoir peur', *Terre Magazine* (the monthly liaison

and information magazine for the Armée de Terre). December 2000–January 2001.

4 Interview in the military prison, cf. *Beyond the Gate* (dir. Jean Baronnet), Arte, Gloria Film, 2004.

5 'I too had a heart' (Rudolf Hoess, *Le Commandant d'Auschwitz parle*).

6 Title of a book by Georges Bernanos (Paris: Grasset, 1931), used differently here.

7 Gitta Sereny, *Into that Darkness, an Examination of Conscience*, New York: Vintage, 1983.

8 Hannah Arendt, *Eichmann in Jerusalem: A Report on the Banality of Evil*, New York: Viking, 1963.

9 *Commandant of Auschwitz: The Autobiography of Rudolf Hoess* (*supra*, note 8, p. 209).

10 *Beyond the Gate*, Arte, Gloria Film, 2004.

11 Duch relates the sequence of events that preceded Lay and San's death, giving the same details that he delivers in writing in his 'Miscellaneous' five years later (cf. Document 1, pp. 141–145).

V. 2009 – THE DEFENDANT

1 Cf. Document 1, *passim*.

2 The traditional Cambodian protective spirits

3 *The Gate*, pp. 218–222. (Folio)

4 Ernst Jünger, *Second Paris Diary*, March 1943.

5 Yves Bonnefoy, *Le lieu d'herbes, le lac au loin*, Paris: 2010, Galilée p. 27.

6 *The Gate*, London: Vintage, 2004, p. 106.

7 Hearing, day 5, 00315759, E1/9.1, 4 April, 2009. See also Document 1, p. 139 and Document 2, pp. 171–174.

8 *The Gate*, Vintage UK edn, p. 115.

9 Document 2, pp. 179–181.

10 I received these Battambang interviews, which were never published, directly from Nate Thayer (*see above*, Chapter IV, note 1). It was found that the recordings were made illegally and could not be distributed.

11 Thierry Cruvellier, *Le Maître des aveux*, Paris: Gallimard, 2011, pp.192–193.

12 *The Gate*, pp. 88–89, and *below*, Document 1, p. 134.

13 Cf. Document 2, pp. 192–193. Nuon Chea was Pol Pot's second in command, the one Duch regarded as the actual person responsible for the massacres, even more than Son Sen; I likened him to the devil in several articles.

14 Cf. Document 2, pp. 198–199.

15 Thierry Cruvellier, *Le maître des aveux*, Paris: Gallimard 2011 (pp. 192–193).

16 Mr François Roux, lawyer for the defence, in his closing statement on 26 November, 2009.

17 Duch's reply to Kerry Hamill's brother, tortured and killed in Tuol.

18 Khieu Samphan, former president of the government of Democratic Kampuchea; Ieng Sary, former Minister of Foreign Affairs; Nuon Chea, former secretary of the Communist Party of Kampuchea; Ieng Thirith, former Minister of Social Affairs.

19 'To find the source of the evil that was enacted at S-21 on a daily basis, we need look no further than ourselves.' David Chandler, *Voices from S-21*, p. 155. Cf. also David Chandler, *S-21 ou le crime impuni des Khmers rouges*, with a preface by François Bizot, Paris: Autrement, 2002, p. 10.

20 Yves Bonnefoy, *Mes Souvenirs d'Arménie*, Paris: 2010, p. 57.

21 'But in our innermost selves, everything is complete.' Johann
   Wolfgang von Goethe, 'Wilhelm Tischbein's Idylls' (1821).

DOCUMENT 1

1 Duch is addressing me using the term *lok*, 'Mister', instead of *mit*,
  'Comrade', which he used in the past.

2 On the importance and sources of this statement, see. François
  Bizot, *La Pureté par les mots*, Paris: EFEO, 1996, pp. 40–45.

3 Chay Kim Hour, alias Hok, former maths teacher and head of the
  executive office for the Southwest Region. Cf. *The Gate*, Vintage
  UK edn, p. 277.

4 President of the 'special zone.'

5 On Serge Thion's clandestine journey to Cambodia, see. Philip
  Short, *Pol Pot: Anatomy of a Nightmare*, New York: John McRae
  Books/Holt, 2005, pp. 326–327.

6 Bernard Philippe Groslier (1926–1986), Angkor's curator.

7 The deputy – the man who met me when I arrived in the camp
  and who I was so scared of (cf. Document 2, p. 199).

8 See Chapter III, 1988 – The Torturer, end note 4, p. 211.

DOCUMENT 2

1 The bailiff came to help me turn the book in the right direction
  and to use the projector.